D0090540

MANAGING YOUR EMOTIONS
INSTEAD OF YOUR EMOTIONS
MANAGING YOU!

MANAGING YOUR EMOTIONS
INSTEAD OF YOUR EMOTIONS MANAGING YOU!

by

Joyce Meyer

A Division of AOL Time Warner Book Group

Warner Books Edition
Copyright © 1997 by Joyce Meyer
Life In The Word, Inc.
P.O. Box 655
Fenton, Missouri 63026
All rights reserved.

Warner Books, Inc., 1271 Avenue of the Americas, New York, NY 10020
Visit our Web site at www.twbookmark.com.

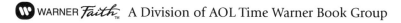 WARNER *Faith*™ A Division of AOL Time Warner Book Group

Printed in the United States of America

First Warner Faith Printing: October 2002
10 9 8 7 6 5 4 3

ISBN: 0-446-53202-9
LCCN: 2002110829

CONTENTS

Many of the thoughts in this book were originally presented in several seminar series I taught on the subject of emotions and emotional health and healing. In those meetings I made it clear to my listeners that the purpose of the presentation was not to teach them how to get rid of emotions, but how to manage emotions.

As I told them, nobody will ever reach the place of not having emotions. Nobody will ever reach a point in life of not experiencing a wide variety of feelings.

For example, no matter how hard you and I may try, we will always have to deal with the emotion of anger, which causes many people a lot of guilt and condemnation. The reason they come under guilt and condemnation is because they have the false idea that as Christians we are never to get angry.

Yet the Bible does not teach that we are never to feel anger. Instead it teaches that when we do get angry, we are not to sin, but rather we are to manage or control our anger in the proper way: **Be ye angry, and sin not: let not the sun go down upon your wrath** (Eph. 4:26 KJV).

There was a time when God gave me a real revelation about that Scripture. I had gotten angry at my husband one day as I was about to leave home to go preach. Guilt and condemnation came over me asking, "How can you go out and preach to others after getting angry like that this morning?"

Of course, I was still angry, so that question bothered me. As I began to meditate on it, the Lord revealed to me this verse in Ephesians which says to be angry and sin not.

God caused me to understand that anger is just an emotion. Like all emotions, it was given to us by God Himself for a reason. If we didn't have the capacity to become angry, we would never know when someone else was mistreating us. That's what anger is for. Like pain, it is there to warn us that something is wrong.

As with all emotions, the problem is Satan tries to use and abuse our anger to lead us into sin.

Many times people come to me for counseling, saying, "I have this deep-seated anger inside me." This anger is often a wound left over from childhood hurts. In that case, the answer is not so much to get rid of the anger, but to get at the root of what is causing it to hang on and cause problems after all these years.

This is part of staying in balance. It is not right to go around feeling angry all the time, any more than it is right to go around feeling pain all the time. But we must remember that we are human beings and are equipped with certain feelings and emotions like anger that were given to us by God for a reason. Our job is not so much to try to get rid of those emotions, but to learn how to manage them.

Another example of emotions is sexual feelings. Imagine for a moment that you are looking through a magazine or a catalog and you spot a photograph of an attractive person of the opposite sex. Suddenly you feel a sexual emotion. Does this mean you are perverted and have something desperately wrong with you? Does it mean you are not really saved — that you don't truly love God or your spouse?

No, it simply means that you are human and subject to all the same emotional feelings and reactions experienced by other human beings. The important thing is how you handle your emotions.

God equips us with all kinds of feelings, including sexual feelings. As Christians, we are not to rid ourselves of those feelings, nor do we need to feel guilty because we have them, but rather we are to learn to vent them properly — in the right way with the right person — with the marriage partner God has given us (the one we love). We are also to learn, with God's help, to keep those feelings under control until we are married.

Romans 6:2 tells us that if we are Christians we have died to sin. It does not tell us that sin is dead! Sin still initially presents itself in the form of temptation and then it becomes a full-blown problem if we give in to the temptation. I recommend reading the sixth chapter of Romans in its entirety. If you do that, you will see that our instruction is to resist sin in the power of the Holy Spirit. We are not told that we will never *feel*, but we are told not to continue offering our bodies as instruments of sin.

It is important to remember that emotions won't disappear and go away. They will always be there. We must not deny their existence or feel guilty because of them. Instead we are to channel them in the right direction. We are to deny the flesh the right to rule us, but we are not to deny that it exists.

As we will see later on, the Bible teaches us to be well-balanced. Often, our problem is that we tend to go from one extreme to another. Either we try not to have any emotions at all, or else we give vent to every emotion we feel whether it is right to do so or not. It seems that the majority of people are either emotional or emotionless. What is really needed is balance — the ability to show emotions when they are positive and helpful, and to control emotions when they are negative and destructive.

When we are angry and frustrated by something in our life, we often take out our anger and frustration on someone else — usually our spouse, children, or someone else with whom we share a close relationship. The problem is not our anger and frustration as much as it is our lack of control.

Another example is patience — or the lack of it. In my natural personality, I have a tendency to be very impatient. I want things done. I want them done right. And, I want them done right away. I don't want to have to tell anyone twice — and certainly not three times!

But the more I read about Jesus and His gentleness, humility, kindness, and longsuffering, the more I desire not to be controlled by impatience. So for a long time I have been working with the Holy Spirit to bring that emotion into proper balance.

The main thing is to understand what emotions are and to recognize that we have them because God gave them to us. Then we need to start dealing with them instead of simply venting and consequently feeling guilty and condemned because of them.

We serve a God Who is pleased with whatever effort we, as believers in Jesus Christ, make to move in His direction. God is not hard to please. He does not expect us to be absolutely perfect. He just expects us to keep moving toward Him and believing in Him, letting Him work with us to bring us into conformity to His will and ways.

The message of these pages is simple: There is nothing wrong with emotions, as long as they are kept under control. The Lord led me to write this book to help you learn to *manage your emotions*.

1
HOW NOT TO BE LED BY YOUR FEELINGS

There are several definitions of the word "emotions." According to Webster's dictionary, the root source of this term is the Latin *ex-movere*, meaning to move away.[1]

I find that definition very interesting because that is what carnal, uncrucified emotions try to do — to move us to follow them away from or out of the will of God.

In fact, that is Satan's plan for our lives — to get us to live by our carnal feelings so we never walk in the Spirit.

The dictionary also says that *emotions* are "a complex, usually strong subjective response...involving physiological changes as a preparation for action."[2] That is true. Because of their complexity, emotions are not easy to explain, which sometimes makes dealing with them difficult.

For example, there are times when the Holy Spirit is leading us to do something, and our emotions become involved, so we get all excited about doing it. The emotional support helps us feel that God really does want us to do the thing. We perceive the emotional support to be confirmation of God's will.

At other times, the Lord will move us to do a certain thing, and our emotions will not want anything to do with what God is revealing to us and asking us to do. They give no support at all.

At those times it is harder to obey God. We are very dependent upon emotional support. If we lack understanding about the fickle nature of emotions, Satan can use them — or the lack of them — to keep us out of God's will. I firmly believe that no person will ever walk in God's will and ultimately in victory if he takes counsel with his emotions.

EMOTIONS OR GOD?

The wise also will hear and increase in learning,
and the person of understanding will acquire skill
and attain to sound counsel [so that he may be able
to steer his course rightly].... Proverbs 1:5

Because there are times when we are allowed to enjoy our emotions and the support they give us, and there are also times when our emotions work against us, it is often hard to teach people how to know when they are hearing from God and when they are listening to their emotions.

Just because we have a "gooey" feeling we are supposed to give something away does not necessarily mean it is the will of God. I love to give things to people. It is really one of the greatest joys of my life, but I have had to learn that giving to people doesn't always help them. Actually, it can hurt them by hindering what God is trying to do in their life.

If, for example, they are not doing their part to take care of what they have, God may let them remain needy until they learn to take care of what they have. But the person who operates out of emotions will see a need and just be moved to meet it without seeking wisdom.

The Bible teaches us in the very first chapter of Proverbs that we are to operate in wise thoughtfulness. If we don't follow this scriptural advice, we can keep a person from growing up and learning to accept personal responsibility.

The other side of the situation also needs to be considered. There may be someone who is not fully mature in the Lord and has much to learn. He is in need, and his need may be the result of not knowing what to do. God may still lead us to help someone in this state, because we all need encouragement while we are growing in the Lord.

We all make messes in our lives through ignorance of God's ways. Even when we begin to learn His ways, it still takes a lot of time to see all the negative situations in our lives turned into positive ones. We can benefit one another greatly by being sensitive to the Holy Spirit's leading to help in various ways. Just being moved emotionally is not being led by the Holy Spirit. *Emotions should always be submitted to wisdom!* If wisdom agrees, then we can go forward with our plan.

Here is an example: We all love our children and know how difficult it is to see them do without things they want and need. If we have the ability to provide those things, most of us want to rescue them out of any difficult situation they are in. This may be very good most of the time. It is good to help our children and to let them know that we will be there for them when they need us. However, rescuing them out of every difficult situation may prevent them from growing up. Struggle is part of the process all of us need in order to mature.

In researching material for a seminar a while back, I read that a baby eaglet, while he is still in the egg, develops a tiny sharp tooth on the end of his beak. He uses this tooth to repeatedly hit the shell until it finally cracks open. This process takes a long time and requires a lot of tenacity. Sometimes well-meaning people try to help by breaking open the shell. When that happens, often the eaglet dies.

Like baby eagles, young people need the experience of the struggle to help prepare them for life. We should help our children, but not to the point of hindering their maturity.

EMOTIONAL PEOPLE

An emotional person is someone who is easily affected with or stirred by emotions. It is good to know ourselves and our personalities. Some people are more emotionally led than others, and knowing this can prevent lots of heartache and pain in life.

Even if we do not fall into the category of an "emotional" person, we each have emotions and are in danger of being led by them. We may get up one morning feeling depressed and follow that feeling throughout the day.

The next day, we may wake up angry — feeling like telling somebody off — and that's what we end up doing. Other times, we may wake up feeling sorry for ourselves and sit in a corner crying all day long.

If we allow them to do so, *feelings* will stir up problems that will cause us to move out of the will of God and into the will of the deceiver, Satan.

I spent many years of my life following how I felt. If I awoke feeling depressed, I was depressed all day. I didn't know at the time that I could *resist* these emotions. Now I realize I can put on the garment of praise as the Bible teaches in Isaiah 61:3. I can sing or play good Christian music — and in doing so — fight against the negative feeling that desires to control me all day.

We must learn to be aware of our emotions and know how to manage them correctly. One way to do that is by recognizing different personality types and knowing how they react differently to similar situations.

Four Basic Personality Types

Just as it is often said that some personality types are more emotional than others, women are thought to have a stronger tendency toward emotionalism than men. According to a teaching that goes far back into history, there are four basic personality types, each of which has an identifying name.

The first type is called *choleric*, which happens to be the category into which I fall. Cholerics are born leaders. Their strong personalities want to be in control. One of the strengths of those who have a choleric personality is that they usually get a lot accomplished. One of their weaknesses is that they have a tendency to be bossy.

Cholerics are normally strongly goal-oriented and motivated by new ideas and challenges. When the Lord gives me a project, I get all stirred up about it and rush to my husband, who has a completely different personality from mine.

Dave is part of the group called *phlegmatic*. Phlegmatics usually show little or no emotion at all. What is interesting is that a choleric often marries a phlegmatic.

In our marriage, our personality differences used to drive us crazy until we saw God's plan in it. Dave is strong in areas where I am weak, and I am strong in areas in which he is weak. I now believe that God brings opposite types together to complement one another, but it took Dave and me a while to learn to accept and operate compatibly with our differences.

To illustrate, I would go to Dave all enthusiastic about something, and his response would be, "We'll see." At times like that, I just wanted to hit him, until I learned to understand him. I was being emotional, and he was being logical. I was looking at the excitement side, and he was looking at the responsibility side of the issue. I used to yell at him, "Can't you ever get excited about anything?"

We would go into dynamic Charismatic churches, and I would emerge from the service saying, "Wow! Did you feel the presence of God in that place?"

Dave would say, "No, I didn't feel a thing." He knew God was present, but he was not basing God's presence on his feelings. For a long time, I thought the man was emotionally dead.

Both of us have changed after years of God's working with us, and we are more balanced now. I am not so emotionally driven, and he shows more excitement when I am genuinely excited about something.

One thing that is good for the people with phlegmatic personalities to remember is that they need to exercise their faith and make an effort to show some emotion. It can be very dull living with an individual who is bland about everything.

If you are a low-key person, you need to stretch yourself on purpose for the sake of others with whom you are in relationship. We are operating in love when we sacrifice ourselves and do what others need us to do.

On the other hand, if you are more like me and tend to get aggressively excited about new things you are involved in, you may need to learn to tone down your emotions and become more of a balanced person. Remember, it is difficult for a more serious and sober person to relate to you because he truly does not feel what you feel. The answer, of course, is balance, as we will discuss later on.

The third personality type is called *sanguine*. This is the most emotional type of all. The sanguine personality is bubbly and seems to bounce through life. It is easy to tell when a sanguine comes into the room. His voice can be heard above everyone else's: "Oh, I'm so excited to be here!"

The sanguine has a tendency to get on the nerves of a choleric — especially mine! I am the serious, goal-oriented type who always has a plan and am moving toward it. When a sanguine comes bouncing in, it often disturbs me. But the sanguine may not even notice. Because he is so full of fun and energy, he is usually oblivious to anything other than having a good time.

Sanguines often marry the fourth type, called *melancholy*. As you can guess, melancholies are those who have the most trouble with depression. They are the deep people — the thinkers — the organizers. They are the ones who are so organized they alphabetize their spice racks. They tie their shoelaces and put them inside their shoes before carefully placing them in the closet. They believe there is a place for everything, and everything should be in its place.

Sanguines are frequently not very disciplined, and this is, of course, very difficult for the melancholy types to handle. Melancholies are really neat people. They always have a plan, but they usually end up married to sanguines who couldn't care less whether there is a plan or not. Even if they did have a plan, sanguines wouldn't remember it for more than five minutes. They are the ones who park their car in a parking lot or garage, and then can't remember where they left it!

Do you think a sanguine would worry about that? Not the lady I knew who did it. She thought it was funny! Now she has a new story to tell at the parties she bubbles into.

As you can see, how you and I react to emotions depends to an extent upon which of these four types best describes our individual personality: choleric, phlegmatic, sanguine, or melancholy. Most of us are a blend of two or more of the personality types.

It really helps to know yourself. There are some good Christian books available on the subject: *Spirit-Controlled Temperament* by Tim LaHaye and *Your Personality Tree* by Florence Littauer.

Always remember that we can learn to control our weaknesses through the power of the Holy Spirit and in doing so become well-balanced individuals who cannot be controlled by Satan.

Emotionalism

The term "emotionalism" is used to describe "a tendency to rely on or place too much value on emotion."[3] Often it is defined as an "excessive display of emotion."

An "emotionalist" is "one whose conduct...is ruled by emotion as opposed to reason."[4]

One project or assignment I always give those who attend my seminars on this subject is to read the book of Proverbs and find all the verses in it that compare emotion to wisdom.

In doing this, they usually learn that one of the differences between wisdom and emotion concerns proper timing.

Wisdom always waits for the right time to act, while emotion always pushes for action right now! Emotionalism is rash. It calls for immediate action. While wisdom calmly looks ahead to determine how a decision will affect the future, emotions are only concerned with what is happening at the moment.

How many times have you said or done something in the heat of emotion, then later experienced deep, deep regret for your rash action?

"Oh, if I had only kept my mouth shut!"

It is amazing the damage that can be done to a relationship by one emotional outburst.

One time, when I was trying to learn to control my mouth and not talk back to my husband, I got so emotional the Lord had to say to me, "Joyce, that's enough! Don't you say another word!" I hurriedly left the room, ran down the hall, and locked myself in the bathroom. I was so upset I buried my face in a towel and screamed into it! Sometimes the strongholds in our flesh become so ingrained, it takes some pretty determined action to break them down. That's why we need to learn to fight against our undisciplined emotions and bring them into submission to the will of God.

FIGHTING EMOTIONS

[Therefore, I do not treat God's gracious gift as something of minor importance and defeat its very purpose]; I do not set aside and invalidate and frustrate and nullify the grace (unmerited favor) of God....Galatians 2:21

At first it won't be easy to overcome emotions. It never is. When you and I initially begin to break ourselves of any habit, we have a struggle on our hands. We have to fight within ourselves, crying out to God, "Lord, help me, help me!" It is so wonderful to know that the Holy Spirit is always with us to help us all the time.

If you know you have given yourself over to some bad habit like emotional eating, when you sit down to the table you have to say within yourself, "Holy Spirit, help me not to overeat." In a restaurant where everybody at your table is ordering dessert, and you can feel yourself starting to waiver, you can cry out inside, "Holy Spirit, help me, help me!"

I have found that if I depend upon my flesh through sheer willpower or determination alone, I will fail every time. But if I am determined to resist temptation by calling on the power of the Holy Spirit, I find the strength I need for success.

I have discovered that the Lord is not going to do everything for us in this life. We can't just find someone to lay hands on us and pray for us to be set free from all our bondages. There is a part we must play with our minds and wills. It takes a combination of faith and action.

The Apostle Paul said that he did not take the grace of God in vain. (Gal. 2:21.) He meant that he did not expect God to do everything for him without doing his part too. God gives us the ability to do what we need to do, but we must choose right action.

The writer of the book of Proverbs tells us: **The beginning of Wisdom is: get Wisdom (skillful and godly Wisdom)! [For skillful and godly Wisdom is the principal thing.] And with all you have gotten, get understanding (discernment, comprehension, and interpretation)** (Prov. 4:7.) In other words, we need to be able to see through the lies Satan speaks to our mind and past the feelings he stirs up within us. We must keep our eyes on the Word of God and do what it says — not what the enemy causes us to feel like doing.

If you are going to be a person who is committed to the Word of God, you will have to learn to be led by the Spirit and not by your emotions.

Whenever an emotion rises up on the inside of me, I test it to see if it is in line with the Word of God. If it is not, the Holy Spirit reveals it to me, and I resist it.

That's how we fight against our emotions — by using our will to make a decision to follow God's Word rather than our feelings.

EMOTIONLESS

Someone who is *emotionless* is "lacking emotion — unable to show emotion; one who feels no emotion, or very little emotion."[5]

Many times when people have been hurt badly in their past, they develop a hard core within and build up high walls without to protect themselves. They may have all the same feelings that others have, but they are unable to show them. Sometimes they may even be so hurt they become callous and unable to feel anything. In either case, there is a real healing needed.

HARDENED AND UNBRIDLED EMOTIONS

So this I say and solemnly testify in [the name of] the Lord [as in His presence], that you must no longer live as the heathen (the Gentiles) do in their perverseness [in the folly, vanity, and emptiness of their souls and the futility] of their minds.

Their moral understanding is darkened and their reasoning is beclouded. [They are] alienated

23

(estranged, self-banished) from the life of God [with no share in it; this is] because of the ignorance (the want of knowledge and perception, the willful blindness) that is deep-seated in them, due to their hardness of heart [to the insensitiveness of their moral nature].

In their spiritual apathy they have become callous and past feeling and reckless and have abandoned themselves [a prey] to unbridled sensuality, eager and greedy to indulge in every form of impurity [that their depraved desires may suggest and demand]. Ephesians 4:17-19

The Lord called my attention to this passage about unbelievers and showed me two things about it. First of all, it says unbelievers are so callous and hard they are past feeling. But in the same verse it says they live by their feelings in sensuality and carnality.

As I meditated on that statement, the Lord showed me that such people are past doing what they should be doing with their feelings.

God gives us feelings for a specific purpose and use in our walk with Him. These people have been hardened to the place they are past using their feelings for the right purpose. Satan has moved them into an area in which they are living riotous lives, doing whatever they feel like doing.

What is the world's philosophy today? "If it feels good, do it!" You and I are not to live that way.

JESUS AND EMOTIONS
๛

For we do not have a High Priest Who is unable to understand and sympathize and have a shared feeling with our weaknesses and infirmities and liability to the assaults of temptation, but One Who has been tempted in every respect as we are, yet without sinning. Hebrews 4:15

According to this verse, Jesus experienced every emotion and suffered every feeling you and I do, yet without sinning. Why did He not sin? Because He did not give in to His wrong feelings. He knew the Word of God in every area of life because He spent years studying it before He began His ministry.

The Bible says that as a child Jesus **...grew and became strong in spirit, filled with wisdom...**(Luke 2:40) so that by the time He was twelve years old, He thought He was old enough to go to the temple in Jerusalem and "be about His Father's business." (Luke 2:41-52.) But He still had years of learning before He entered His full-time ministry.

You and I will never be able to say no to our feelings if we don't have within us a strong knowledge of the Word of God. Jesus had the same feelings we do, but He never sinned by giving in to them.

When I am hurt by someone and I feel angry or upset, it is such a comfort to me to be able to lift my face and hands and voice to the Lord saying, "Jesus, I am so glad that You understand what I am feeling right now and that You don't condemn me for feeling this way. I don't want to give vent to my emotions. Help me, Lord, to get over them. Help me to forgive those who have wronged me and not slight them, avoid them, or seek to pay them back for the harm they have done me. Help me not to live under condemnation in thinking that I shouldn't be feeling this way."

It is not a matter of just thinking, "I shouldn't be feeling this way." It is a matter of crying out to God and functioning in the fruit of the Spirit called self-control. (Gal. 5:23.)

You and I don't have to feel condemned because we have bad feelings. Jesus understands. His main concern is that we come to the point where we are like Him: humble, gentle, meek, and lowly. He wants us to develop compassion, understanding, and softness of heart.

Because I was hurt really badly in my childhood, I developed a hard core and built up high walls around myself for self-protection, just like those I have mentioned. I became hard and calloused on the inside. But I learned and am still learning that any kind of personality, no matter how hurt or hurting, can be presented and projected in a kind, gentle way.

No matter what our past experiences or our present feelings, we are to be compassionate toward others. We are to rejoice with those who rejoice, but we are also to weep with those who weep. (Rom. 12:15.)

One of the things Jesus imparted to people and imparts to us today, and one of the things we need to impart to others, is not hardness, but understanding.

No matter what anybody does or has done to us, we need to convey to them the message: "I understand what you are going through. I understand how you feel. But also let me tell you what the Word of God says. You don't have to stay the way you are." Hurting people hurt people, but love can heal and change them.

It is obvious what Satan wants us to do. He wants us to develop hardness and callousness within us so that we *cannot* feel or be sensitive to the needs of others.

God wants us to be more sensitive to the feelings and needs of others and less sensitive to our own feelings and needs. He wants us to deposit ourselves in His hands and let Him take care of us while we are practicing being kind and compassionate and sensitive to other people.

As believers, we are not to be led by our feelings, but we are to be moved by them to show compassion and understanding to those in need. That is the right purpose and use of feelings and emotions, **...so that we may also be able to comfort (console and encourage) those who are in any kind of trouble or distress, with the comfort (consolation and encouragement) with which we ourselves are comforted (consoled and encouraged) by God** (2 Cor. 1:4).

FEELINGS OR DECISION?

...being in an agony [of mind], He prayed [all the] more earnestly and intently, and His sweat became like great clots of blood dropping down upon the ground. Luke 22:44

Remember, feelings are part of the soul which is often said to be composed of the mind, will, and emotions.

When we are born again, we are not told to stop thinking. We are just told to start thinking a new way.

When we are born again, we are not told to stop deciding, to stop desiring, we are just told to surrender our will to God and decide to do what He desires, according to the leading of the Holy Spirit.

The same is true with emotions. When we are born again, we are not told to stop *feeling*. We are just told to learn how to express those feelings in the right way.

Jesus did not *feel* like going to the cross, but He resisted against operating by His feelings. He subjected His emotions to His heavenly Father.

In the Garden of Gethsemane, Jesus went through agony of soul in His efforts to resist the temptation to do what He *felt* like doing rather than what He knew was God's will for Him.

TESTING THE EMOTIONS

Oh, let the wickedness of the wicked come to an end, but establish the [uncompromisingly] righteous [those upright and in harmony with You]; for You, Who try the hearts and emotions and thinking powers, are a righteous God. Psalm 7:9

Here in Psalm 7:9 and also in Revelation 2:23 **(...I am He Who searches minds (the thoughts, *feelings*, and purposes) and the [inmost] hearts...)** we read that God is a God Who tries emotions. What does the word *try* mean in this context? It means to test until purified.[6]

A few years ago, as I was praying, God said to me, "Joyce, I am going to test your emotions." I had never heard of anything like that. I didn't know these Scriptures were even in the Bible. So I went on my way.

About six months later I just suddenly seemed to become an emotional wreck. I cried for no reason. Everything hurt my feelings.

I thought, "What is the problem here? What's going on?"

Then the Lord reminded me of what He had said to me earlier, "I am going to test your emotions." He led me to Psalm 7:9 and Revelation 2:23 and caused me to understand what He was doing for my own good.

No matter who you are, there will be periods of time in which you feel more emotional than usual. You may wake up one morning and feel like breaking down and crying for no reason. That may last a week or it may last longer. You may think, "What is my problem?"

During those times you have to be careful because your feelings will get hurt very easily. The slightest thing will set you off.

There were times in my life when I would go to bed praying, feeling as sweet as could be, then wake up the next morning like I had stayed up all night eating nails! I would get up in such a foul mood that if anyone came near me or crossed me, I felt like hitting them on the head!

What should we do when we start feeling that way? First of all, we shouldn't start getting under condemnation. Number two, we shouldn't even try to figure out what is happening. What we should do is simply say, "This is one of those times when my emotions are being tried. I'm going to trust God and learn to control them."

How are you and I ever going to learn to control ourselves emotionally unless God allows us to go through some trying times?

Remember, the Bible says that God will never allow any more to come upon us than we are able to bear. (1 Cor. 10:13.) If the Lord does not allow such testing times to come upon us, we will never learn how to deal with Satan when he brings them upon us — which he will sooner or later.

Trying times are learning times.

Emotions and Fatigue

But he himself went a day's journey into the
wilderness and came and sat down under a lone

broom or juniper tree and asked that he might
die. He said, It is enough; now, O Lord, take
away my life; for I am no better than my fathers.
1 Kings 19:4

I have often heard that after a person goes through a real
emotional high, he will usually bottom out with an emotional
low.

We see this in the life of Elijah the prophet in the book of
1 Kings. One day he is on Mt. Carmel making a fool of the priests
of Baal, calling down fire from heaven, at the height of his
emotion. The next day we see him out in the desert sitting under
a juniper tree asking God to let him die because he feels so
depressed.

In my own life, I have noticed when I minister in a series of
meetings, I spend everything I have spiritually, emotionally, and
mentally, praying for people and meeting their needs. I get so
excited when I see what God is doing through those meetings,
my radio and television broadcasts, and other outreaches we are
involved in.

But then when I return from something exciting like that to
normal, everyday life, it is almost too much to bear. Who wants to
go from casting out demons one day to normal household chores
the next?

Often we get the idea, "Oh, if I could just stay on this
emotional high forever!" But God knows we couldn't stand it. A
lot of emotional highs and lows wear us out emotionally as well
as mentally and physically.

When I came home after those ministry trips, I couldn't
understand what was wrong with me. I would go through the
house rebuking Satan, when the only thing wrong was that I was

tired — physically, mentally, and emotionally drained. Like Elijah in the desert, I didn't need to fight the enemy, I needed to rest and recuperate.

When you get like that, don't do like Elijah and get down on yourself. Don't start thinking what a miserable person you are. Don't moan and groan about how happy you were yesterday but how terrible you feel today. Don't start complaining to the Lord about how worthless you feel.

Do you know what I do when I get like that? I say, "Lord, I'm feeling down right now, so I'm going to have to just rest and build myself back up again. I'm going to spend time with You, Lord, and let You strengthen me."

MANIC DEPRESSION

The psychological term used to describe people who go from one emotional extreme to another is "manic depressive."

A young woman in one of our meetings once told me that her husband was a manic depressive. She said that for three months he would be on an emotional high and be really creative. In his business, he would buy and sell, invest large sums of money, and be tremendously successful. When he came down from that emotional high, he would go into deep depression that might last for as long as six months!

Medical science at one time only tried to bring up the emotional lows for people with manic depression. When they were enjoying an emotional high, nothing was done for them. According to an article I recently read, it has now been discovered that the attempt must be made to bring down the extreme highs. Health experts are learning that balance is the key.

We have always applauded high emotions and been critical of lows. Actually both extreme ends are wrong.

Most of us will never have problems with manic depression, but we can learn a principle from how they are treated, and we can understand that it isn't good enough to simply resist depression, we must also resist the temptation to get so emotionally high that it leaves us exhausted and open prey for the devil.

None of us can live on the mountaintop all the time. There are going to be days when we are up and days when we feel down. Emotions are fickle, and they fluctuate frequently for no apparent reason. What we need to learn is how to manage both ends of the extreme.

One thing that is important for stable emotional health is honesty — with self and with others. People who are close to us can sense when we are struggling emotionally. I have found it is best for me and my family if I am honest with them about what is going on with me. At those times when I have felt myself sliding toward anger, depression, or any negative emotion, I have told my family, "My emotions are going haywire today, so if I'm quiet, just don't pay any attention to me for a while."

We must remember that what we hide still has power over us, but when we bring things out in the open, they begin losing their grip immediately. John 8:32 teaches us that the truth will make us free. James 5:16 encourages us to confess our faults to one another so that we may be healed and restored to a spiritual tone of mind and heart.

I found that if I tried to protect my spiritual reputation by pretending that nothing was wrong with me, all it did was bring confusion to my entire family. They might begin to imagine that

I was angry with them for some reason. Then they would become upset, trying to reason out what they might have done to upset me. We were all a lot better off if I simply told the truth.

I tried to learn to be quiet during those times.

We have a tendency to say things when we are emotionally upset that we regret later. We have a responsibility to our family members and others with whom we spend a lot of time to avoid keeping them guessing about what's going on with us.

Here is a good example: One of the members of our road team who is normally very talkative and bubbly suddenly became very quiet and almost withdrawn. Several of the other team members noticed it and came to Dave and me saying, "What's wrong with _____?" They thought she was angry about something or with someone on the travel crew.

When I spoke with her, she was simply having some health problems. She had recently gone for some medical tests and was anxiously awaiting the results. She said, "I always get quiet and just pray when I'm dealing with something like this."

I told her that getting quiet and praying was the thing to do, but that it might be good the next time to just mention to everyone that she was dealing with something personal and not to think anything about it if she seemed quiet. By doing so, we can prevent the devil from placing negative things in other people's imaginations about the situation.

People respect us if we are open and straightforward. I learned this truth with my family, and it saved all of us a lot of anxiety.

Remember that the devil will use our emotions to bring us under guilt and condemnation, but God often uses them to test or try us so that we come forth from our emotional upheavals stronger and better able to control them than ever before.

The trick is to learn not to give in or cater to emotions. I spent many years being up and down emotionally, but now I am very stable. God helps us as we continue trusting Him and following the leadership of the Holy Spirit.

The Price for Catering to Emotions
~

> So then those who are living the life of the flesh [catering to the appetites and impulses of their carnal nature] cannot please or satisfy God, or be acceptable to Him. Romans 8:8

The Amplified Bible tells us that to live by the flesh is to cater to the appetites and impulses of the carnal or fleshly nature.

Now we have all been at banquets and other events which were catered. It is always fun to be catered to, to have our wants and needs met immediately and fully by someone else. But there is always a price to be paid for that kind of service.

The same is true in the area of emotions. There is a price we must pay for falling into the position of catering to the desires and demands of our emotions — what the Bible calls our "flesh."

> Now the mind of the flesh [which is sense and reason without the Holy Spirit] is death [death that comprises all the miseries arising from sin, both here and hereafter]. But the mind of the [Holy] Spirit is life and [soul] peace [both now and forever]. Romans 8:6

This means that if you and I follow the dictates and demands of our flesh — our unbridled emotions — we will have a price to pay. Why?

> ...because the mind of the flesh [with its carnal thoughts and purposes] is hostile to God, for it does

not submit itself to God's Law; indeed it cannot.
Romans 8:7

Part of the price we must pay for catering to our emotions is not being able to live the Spirit-filled life:

> For those who are according to the flesh and are controlled by its unholy desires set their minds on and pursue those things which gratify the flesh, but those who are according to the Spirit and are controlled by the desires of the Spirit set their minds on and seek those things which gratify the [Holy] Spirit. Romans 8:5

The Bible clearly teaches that the flesh is opposed to the Spirit, and the Spirit is opposed to the flesh. They are continually antagonistic to each other. This means that we cannot be led by our emotions and still be led by the Holy Spirit, so we have to make a choice.

Now when the Bible says that those who cater to their emotions cannot please or satisfy God or be acceptable to Him, it does not mean that God doesn't love them.

You and I can be in a terrible emotional mess and still be loved by our heavenly Father. The fact that we are having emotional problems does not mean we are not going to heaven. It just means God is not pleased with our lifestyle. Why? Because it puts Him in a position in which He cannot do for us what He would like to do.

As I have mentioned previously, we all want our children to be blessed and to share in our inheritance. But if one of our children chooses to follow a lifestyle of unbridled sensuality, we will not be inclined to entrust our inheritance to him because we know he will just squander and waste it on "riotous living," fulfilling the "lust of the flesh." When the Apostle Paul says God is not pleased with those who live by the flesh rather than by His Spirit, I believe Paul means they cannot be trusted with God's best.

Ordinary Impulses

For you are still [unspiritual, having the nature] of the flesh [under the control of ordinary impulses]. For as long as [there are] envying and jealousy and wrangling and factions among you, are you not unspiritual and of the flesh, behaving yourselves after a human standard and like mere (unchanged) men? 1 Corinthians 3:3

In his letter to the church in Corinth, the Apostle Paul called the Corinthians unspiritual because they were living not by the Spirit of God but by their own human nature, which was under the control of "ordinary impulses."

Notice Paul did not say these people were unspiritual because they had ordinary impulses, but because they were *under the control* of ordinary impulses. Instead of controlling their impulses, they were allowing their impulses to control them.

I define *impulse* as a sudden urge that compels a person to take action, or an inherent, irrational tendency. I think an impulsive person is one who tends to act on emotion rather than on logic or wisdom.

We often speak of "impulse buying," which, of course, refers to buying something without really giving careful thought to the purchase.

Paul says that being impulsive, being led by ordinary impulses rather than by the Spirit of God, leads to all kinds of evils such as jealousy, envy, strife — in short, all the things that cause divisions and factions among us.

EMOTIONS AS THE ENEMY
ॐ

Watchman Nee made two important statements about emotions in his book, *Spiritual Man*: 1) "Emotion may be denominated the most formidable enemy to the life of a spiritual Christian," and 2) "He therefore who lives by emotion lives without principle."[7]

What he was saying was the same thing Paul is saying in this passage. We cannot be spiritual — that is, walk in the Spirit — and be led by emotions.

Emotions will not go away, but we can learn to manage them. We all have emotions, and we must deal with them, but we cannot trust them! Why? Because emotions are our greatest enemy. More than anything, Satan uses our emotions against us to keep us from walking in the Spirit.

We know the mind is the battlefield — the place where the battle is waged between the Spirit and the soul. I have read that when emotion pulsates, the mind becomes deceived, and conscience is denied its standard of judgment.

People often ask me, "How can I know for sure whether I'm hearing from God or from my emotions?"

I believe the answer is to learn to wait. Emotions urge us toward haste. They tell us that we have to do something, and we must do it right now! But godly wisdom tells us to wait until we have a clear picture of what it is we are to do and when we are to do it.

What we all need to do is develop the capacity to back away and view our situation from God's perspective. We need to be able to make decisions based on what we *know* rather than on what we *feel*.

Many times we say, "Well, I *feel* that God wants me to do this or that." In reality what we are saying is we sense in our spirit that the Lord is telling us to do or not do something. We are not talking about operating by our own emotions, but by what we perceive spiritually to be the will of God for us in that situation.

Whenever we are faced with a decision, we need to ask ourselves: "Am I making this decision according to my feelings or according to the will of God?"

Let me give you an example from my own personal life.

EMOTIONAL DISCERNMENT

⌁

我们行事为人
是凭着信心,不
是凭着眼见。"

For we walk by faith [we regulate our lives and conduct ourselves by our conviction or belief respecting man's relationship to God and divine things, with trust and holy fervor; thus we walk] not by sight or appearance. 2 Corinthians 5:7

My husband Dave and I have a certain way we handle our money. I get an allowance each week, and so does he. I usually save my money to buy clothes and other things I want or need.

One time I had about $375 saved to buy a good watch, which I had to do about once a year since I have a lot of acid in my skin. I wanted to buy a good, 14-karat gold watch, so the band would not discolor.

Because I had been shopping for a watch for a while and

discovered that the type I wanted would cost about eight or nine hundred dollars, I was saving my money toward that goal.

One day Dave and I were in the mall and happened to stop at a jewelry store where I saw a watch that was only gold-plated but was really very pretty. It matched my ring and seemed to be just what I was looking for. It fit my arm perfectly so it wouldn't have had to have been cut down. Not only that, but the clerk offered to mark it down from $395 to $316. So my emotions said, "YES! That's exactly what I want!"

But then my husband said, "Well, now, you know, it's not 14-karat gold."

So I asked the clerk, "How long do you think the gold-plating will last?"

"Well, it could last from five to ten years," he said, "depending on how much acid you have in your skin."

I turned to Dave and said. "Oh, my. I really like that watch. What should I do?"

"It's your money," he answered.

"I'll tell you what I'm going to do," I told the clerk. "You hold it for me for half an hour. I'm going to walk around the mall for a bit. If I want the watch, I'll come back within thirty minutes."

So Dave and I walked around the mall for a while. As we did so, we passed a dress shop. Because I needed a couple of new outfits, I went in and found a really nice suit. I tried it on, and it fit perfectly. I loved it.

"That's a nice suit," Dave said. "You really ought to get it."

I looked at the price tag and saw that it read $279. "No wonder it looks so good on me," I replied. But I really wanted that suit!

After a while I put the suit back in the rack.

"Aren't you going to buy it?" David asked.

"No," I answered. "I'm not going to buy it either. I'm going to think about it."

Actually there were three things I wanted. I wanted the watch, I wanted the suit, and I wanted not to be broke. I wanted to have some money on hand to buy little things I needed from time to time and to be able to do some things I enjoyed like taking my kids out for lunch now and then.

What did I do? I applied wisdom. I decided to wait. The watch would have taken all of my savings and would still not have been what I really needed. The suit was beautiful, but it also would have taken most of my savings. Since it was long-sleeved, I wouldn't have been able to wear it until the next fall. It would have hung in my closet for a long time.

The best thing, I decided, was to keep my money and wait until I was sure what I wanted most.

I really learned a lesson from that experience. I had peace about my decision. As much as I would have enjoyed either the watch or the suit, I knew I had done the right thing.

It turned out that later on my husband bought me both the watch and the suit — plus a ring to match! It all worked out beautifully because I was willing to listen to reason and apply wisdom rather than being controlled by my emotions.

If we are willing to learn to control our emotions, God will bless us.

I am not saying that if you will delay every decision, someone else will make it for you and you will get everything you want and more. I *am* saying that usually the wisest course is: when in doubt, don't!

When faced with any difficult decision, wait until you have a clear answer before taking a step that you may regret. Emotions are wonderful, but they must not be allowed to take precedence over wisdom and knowledge. Remember: control your emotions, don't let them control you.

2
HEALING OF DAMAGED EMOTIONS, PART 1
෫

Healing of emotional wounds is a process, not something that takes place all at once or overnight. It requires an investment of time and diligent obedience to God's commands.

I realize from my own experience that it often seems that no progress is being made at all. You may feel you have so many problems you are getting absolutely nowhere.

But you are!

You have to keep in mind that even though you have a long way to go, you have also come a long way. The solution is to thank God for the progress you have made thus far and to trust Him to lead you on to eventual victory — one step at a time.

ONE STEP AT A TIME
෫

In my oral presentations on this subject I like to hold up several different-colored shoestrings tied together in a knot. I tell my audience, "This is you when you first start the process of transformation with God. You're all knotted up. Each knot represents a different problem in your life. Untangling those knots and straightening out those problems is going to take a bit of time and effort, so don't get discouraged if it doesn't happen all at once."

All of us have many of the same types of problems, but God doesn't deal with all of them at the same time or all of us in the same way. The Lord may be dealing with one person about his mouth, somebody else about his selfishness, and someone else about his anger or bitterness.

If you want to receive emotional healing from God and come into an area of wholeness, you must realize that healing is a process and allow the Lord to deal with you and your problems in His own way and in His own time. Your part is to cooperate with Him in whatever area He chooses to start dealing with you first.

You may want to work on one thing, and God may want to start with something else. If you pursue your own agenda, you will soon learn there is no anointing for that problem. The grace of God is not there to deliver you outside of His timing.

I tell people in my seminars, "Being convicted by the message you hear in this meeting doesn't mean you are to go out and set up some kind of ten-point plan for dealing with that situation. First you must pray and ask God to begin to work in that area of your life. Then you must cooperate with Him as He does it."

As God deals with each of us in one specific area at a time, it may take anywhere from one hour to several years. In my own case, the Lord dealt with me for one solid year to get me to understand He loves me.

I will never forget it. I needed that foundation in my life. I desperately needed to know how much God loved me personally, not just when I had done what I thought I was supposed to do, but all the time — whether I "deserved" His love or not.

I needed to know God loved me unconditionally and His love was not something I could buy with works or good behavior.

As part of the process, I began to get up every morning saying, "God loves me!" Even when I did something wrong, I would say, "God loves me!" When I would have trials or problems, I would say it, again and again: "God loves me!" Every time Satan tried to steal my assurance of that love, I would say it over and over: "God loves me! He loves me!"

I would read books about God's unconditional, unending love. I dwelled on it continually until I had that foundational truth firmly imbedded in my mind and heart: "God loves me!" Through the process of continual study and meditation in this area, I became rooted and grounded in God's love as the Apostle Paul encourages us to do in Ephesians 3.

One of our problems is that in our modern, instantaneous society we tend to jump from one thing to another. We have come to expect everything to be quick and easy. We won't stick with a problem until we see a breakthrough and know that we have victory in that area.

The Lord is not like that. He never gets in a hurry, and He never quits. He will deal with us about one particular thing, and then He will let us rest for a while — but not too long. Soon He will come back and begin to work on something else. He will continue until, one by one, our knots are all untied.

It sometimes seems you are not making any progress because the Lord is untying your knots one at a time. It may be hard, and it make take time, but if you will "stick with the program," sooner or later you will see the victory and experience the freedom you have wanted so long.

In some things I experienced freedom in a few months or a year, but there was one area in my life which took fourteen long years to overcome. Now you may not be as stubborn and hard-headed as I was, so it may not take you that long to break the stronghold holding you in bondage. The important thing to remember is: no matter how long it takes, never give up, and never quit — keep at it!

KEEP PRESSING ON

The main thing God asks or requires we do to bring about the answer to our problems is to believe and keep pressing on. Study the Word of God and spend time with Him.

What else can we do?

Just because we have a knot in our life does not mean we are able to untie it ourselves. Some knots are harder than others to untie. In fact, if we are not careful we can even make them worse than they were. So often in our own efforts to untangle our knots all we do is make matters worse.

At one time in my life I became so entangled in my problems and my futile efforts to untangle them I was no good to myself or anybody else.

But once I learned to let the Lord handle the problems and just cooperate with Him, things began to work much better. Now I am free in Jesus and am able to help others who are as bound and tangled as I was.

PROBLEMS PEOPLE MANIFEST

There are people who have been severely damaged emotionally. I have a feeling that most of us at one time have been or will be part of that group in one way or another, so let's look at some of these problems.

Some people experience feelings of unworthiness. They have a shame-based self-hatred, a sense of self-rejection, an inner voice that tells them they are no good, that something is wrong with them.

For years I walked around with the nagging thought, "What's wrong with me?"

Isn't it strange that when we are born again, the first thing the Lord wants to give us is His righteousness through His blood so we can stop asking what's wrong with us and start confessing what's right with us now that we are in Christ?

Other people become perfectionists. They are always trying to prove their worth and gain love and acceptance through performance. These people always struggle to do a little bit better in the hope that someone will love and accept them more.

Still others are supersensitive. Do you recall what the Apostle Paul says about love in 1 Corinthians 13:5 ...**it is not touchy....**

Are you "touchy"? Would you like to be delivered from super-sensitivity? If so, part of the answer is to face the fact that if you are touchy, the problem is not with those who constantly offend you or hurt your feelings, but it is with you and your super-sensitive nature. Being secure will heal you from being touchy.

One of the things that helped me in this area was a simple statement made to me years ago by a lady who was reading a book on this subject. She told me, "You know, the book I'm reading says that 95 percent of the time when people hurt your feelings, they didn't intend to do so."

That means that if you get your feelings hurt easily, it's

because you choose to. The good news is that you can also choose not to.

I really encourage you to lay aside supersensitivity. You will feel so much better about yourself and others.

I know. I used to get my feelings hurt and wounded if my husband didn't buy me a birthday present or do something else I thought he ought to do to show he loved and appreciated me. If he failed to compliment me when I thought he ought to, I got my feelings hurt.

If you walk into a room and don't get the attention you think you deserve, do you get hurt? Do you feel that others don't esteem you the way they should? If so, you need to place that problem into God's hands and let Him untie that knot of supersensitivity.

One of the things that has helped me tremendously over the past few years is learning to place myself into God's hands and let Him work out things for the best. I try to abandon myself to Him and trust Him to get me what He wants me to have.

In short, I am learning not to look to other people to meet my needs, but rather to look to the Lord to fulfill my needs as He knows best for me.

It is interesting that people who are supersensitive about what others do to them are often totally insensitive to what they do to others.

I was like that. I was supersensitive and yet hard to get along with because I was so insecure.

Many times people are supersensitive because they have been hurt in the past, and so their bruised emotions are easily pained. That's why they are so touchy.

I was that way. Like many people, because I did not get the love I needed for much of my life, I kept trying to get other people to make me happy. When I married, I became a suffocator. Because love and affection had been denied to me, I tended to suffocate anyone who showed me any fondness or attention at all.

I learned that in a marriage relationship, we must allow our partner some liberty. We must get rid of the fear of man and develop instead a reverential fear and awe of God.

Why do some of us have such a tremendous fear of what somebody else thinks of us? The reason is that we have a poor self-image. Do we become any less valuable or worthy in the eyes of God because of someone else's negative opinion of us? Of course not, but we feel less valuable unless we are secure in who we are in Christ.

People who have a great deal of fear of others are good candidates to come under a controlling spirit. We have to be so careful in this area.

Many times people who suffer from poor self-esteem allow themselves to be controlled by someone who promises to show them love or acceptance. They allow themselves to be manipulated like a puppet on a string. They are afraid to break the string because they are fearful of losing the attention they receive from the controller. They fear loneliness.

Then there are those who, because of emotional hurts, become controllers and manipulators themselves. I was one of them.

When I got married, because of my past hurts I had a very hard time submitting to my husband in the Lord, as the Bible teaches. (Eph. 5:22; Col. 3:18) I was afraid if I submitted to him and allowed him to exercise any control over me, he would hurt me.

Dave kept telling me, "Joyce, I'm not going to hurt you! Don't you understand that I love you and that the decisions I make are best for you? God has given me that job."

But I couldn't see that for a long time. I couldn't imagine anybody caring enough for me to make decisions that would benefit me in any way. I thought if I allowed anybody to exercise any degree of control over my life, he would take advantage of me and do what was best for him, not for me. There are people who will do that, but Dave was not one of them. God is asking us to trust Him and believe that if people treat us unjustly, He will vindicate us.

When we have been hurt in the past, we tend to drag our wounds into our new relationships. One of the things God wants to do for us is help us learn to function in the new relationships we have developed, rather than ruin them because of the bad experiences we have had in the past.

Then there are the addictive behaviors: alcoholism, drug addictions, food addictions, spending addictions, and on and on.

If you suffer from any of these types of emotional illnesses, God wants to heal you. He wants to heal you from a sense of unworthiness, from shame and self-hatred and self-rejection, from addictive behaviors, from supersensitivity and fear and the labor of being a perfectionist, always trying to please God.

One time the Lord said to me, "Joyce, I'm not nearly as hard to please as people think I am."

God does not require that you and I be perfect. If we could be perfect, it would not have been necessary for God to send Jesus, the Perfect Sacrifice, for us.

God has the marvelous ability to love us in the midst of our imperfections. He wants to heal us of our emotional fears and weaknesses and addictions. But in order for Him to do so, we must be willing to be helped.

BE WILLING TO RECEIVE HELP
᠅

...I am the Way.... John 14:6

Many people are hurting so badly, and they are crying out for help. The *problem* is, they are not willing to receive the help they need from God.

The *truth* is, no matter how much we may want or need help, we are never going to receive it until we are willing to do things God's way.

It is amazing how many times we want help, but we want God to do it *our* way. God wants us to do it *His* way.

In John 14:6, Jesus said, "I am the Way." I received a really good understanding of that truth as I was preparing this message.

What Jesus meant when He said, "I am the Way," is that He has a certain way of doing things, and if we will submit to *His* way, everything will work out for us. But so often we wrestle and struggle with Him, trying to get Him to do things our way. It just won't work.

For example, in my ministry we constantly tell people, "You have got to be in the Word of God — you have got to read and study the Bible daily." Otherwise they won't know what God's way is and how to receive help from Him.

How many times have people stood in front of me at the altar and told me all kinds of terrible things that are going on in their lives and how badly they are hurting — and I want to help them

— yet they absolutely refuse to do what they are told to do to receive the help they need.

I ask them, "Are you in the Word?"

"Well, not really."

"Do you go to church?"

"No, I don't always get there."

"How often do you go to spiritual meetings like this one?"

"Every now and then, maybe once a year."

"Do you listen to teaching tapes?"

"Oh, I have four or five, but I've never listened to them."

It is not always like that, but it is usually just a hit or miss situation. The point is that too often people are trying to find some other way to get help rather than by doing things God's way.

The Bible plainly teaches that if we will learn and act on the Word, God will bless our lives.

Let me give you an example. The Bible teaches that we are to live in harmony and peace with others and to forgive those who have done us wrong. If we refuse to do that, what hope do we have of receiving what we need?

If we don't do what we can do, then God won't do what we can't do. If we will do what we can do, God will do what we can't do. It's just that simple.

I realize that one reason we don't always do what we are told to do in the Word of God is because it is hard to act on the Word sometimes instead of acting according to our feelings.

I remember how difficult it was for me the first time the Lord told me I had to go to my husband and tell him I was sorry for being rebellious against him. I thought I would die on the spot! My flesh screamed and ranted and raved. Because of the way I had been mistreated in my younger days, I had a hard time submitting to anyone, especially men. I thought since I finally had some control over my life I wasn't about to "bow my knee" to anybody! I wasn't about to show what was, to me at least, a "sign of weakness."

Now I realize the Lord was asking me to show meekness, strength under control,[1] and not weakness, submission to domination.

The world will tell us that if we humble ourselves, apologize for our wrongs, and do the things necessary for peace, we are being weak and letting others walk all over us. But God says it is meekness not weakness. Whenever God looks for someone to use, He always looks for a meek person. Only a meek person will consistently obey God.

The Bible says that Moses was the meekest man on the face of the earth when God called him to do the job He had set aside for him. (Num. 12:3.) All we have to do today is what Moses had to do — obey.

OBEY THE WORD

> But be doers of the Word [obey the message],
> and not merely listeners to it, betraying yourselves
> [into deception by reasoning contrary to the Truth].
> James 1:22

I recall a woman who attended one of my seminars. She had a lot of emotional wounds that had left her insecure and fearful. She desperately wanted to be free, but nothing seemed to work for her.

At the conclusion of the seminar she told me that she now understood why she had never experienced any progress. She said,

"Joyce, I sat with a group of ladies who all had a lot of the same problems in the past that I did. They also had emotional problems but step by step God had been delivering them. As I listened to them, I heard them say, 'God led me to do this, and I did it. Then He led me to another thing, and I did it.' I realized as I sat there that God had also told me to do the same things He told them to do. The only difference was they did what He said to do, and I didn't."

To receive from God what He has promised us in His Word, we must obey the Word. Yes, we must receive the Word, but then we must become doers of the Word and not hearers only.

We need to go to Bible study and church to hear the Word, but we also need to go out into the world and put that Word into practice in our daily lives. There will be times when doing what the Word says is not easy, times when we don't *feel* like doing what it tells us to do.

Obeying the Word requires consistency and diligence. It can't be hit or miss. We can't just do it for a while to see if it works. There must be a dedication and commitment to do the Word whatever the outcome.

I have been dealing with this issue for a long, long time, and believe me when I say those who do things God's way get the victory!

"Yes," you may say, "but I have been doing the Word for a long time, and I still don't have the victory!"

Then do it some more. Nobody knows exactly how long it is going to take for the Word to begin to work in his life. But I assure you that if you keep at it, sooner or later it will work.

God's way works! And there is no other way that does.

I know it is often a struggle to "keep on keeping on" — especially when it seems that nothing is happening. I know it's a fight. I know Satan tries to keep you out of the Word, and once you do get into the Word, he tries everything in his power to keep you from putting the Word into practice in your life. I also know that once you do start putting the Word into practice, he does everything he can to make you think it won't work.

That's why you must keep at it. Ask God to help by giving you a desire to get into His Word and to do it no matter how hard it is or how long it takes to produce any results in your life.

DO YOU WANT TO GET WELL?

There was a certain man there who had suffered with a deep-seated and lingering disorder for thirty-eight years.

When Jesus noticed him lying there [helpless], knowing that he had already been a long time in that condition, He said to him, Do you want to become well? [Are you really in earnest about getting well?] John 5:5,6

Isn't this an amazing question for Jesus to ask this poor man who had been sick for thirty-eight long years: "Do you really want to become well?"

That is the Lord's question to you as you read these words right now: "Do you really want to become well?"

Do you know there are people who really don't want to get well? They just want to talk about their problem. Are you one of those people? Do you really want to get well or do you just want to talk about your problem?

Sometimes people get addicted to having a problem. It becomes their identity, their life. It defines everything they think and say and do. All their being is centered around it.

If you have a "deep-seated and lingering disorder," the Lord wants you to know that it does not have to be the central focal point of your entire existence. He wants you to trust Him and cooperate with Him as He leads you to victory over that problem one step at a time.

Don't try to use your problem as a means of getting attention or sympathy or pity.

When I used to complain to my husband, he would tell me, "Joyce, I'm not going to feel sorry for you."

"I'm not trying to get you to feel sorry for me," I would protest.

"Yes, you are," he would say. "And I'm not going to do it, because if I do, you will never get over your problems."

That used to make me so mad I could have beaten him to a pulp. We get angry at those who tell us the truth. And the truth is that before we can get well, we must really *want* to be well — body, soul, and spirit. We must want to enough that we are willing to hear and accept truth.

God works differently with individuals. Each of us must learn to follow God's personal plan for us. Whatever our problem may be, God has promised to meet our need and to repay us for our loss. Facing truth is the key to unlocking prison doors that may have held us in bondage.

THE JUSTICE OF GOD

Instead of your [former] shame you shall have
a twofold recompense; instead of dishonor and

reproach [your people] shall rejoice in their portion. Therefore in their land they shall possess double [what they had forfeited]; everlasting joy shall be theirs. Isaiah 61:7

The word *recompense* means "repayment."[2] So when the prophet says that the Lord will recompense us for our shame, dishonor, and reproach, he means that God will make it up to us for all the hurts we have experienced in life.

The Bible says, **Beloved, never avenge yourselves, but leave the way open for [God's] wrath; for it is written, Vengeance is Mine, I will repay (requite), says the Lord** (Rom. 12:19).

One of the greatest mistakes we make is trying to avenge ourselves, to get even, to bring the scales of justice into balance, rather than trusting God to do that for us. If we try to do it ourselves, we only wind up making a huge mess.

When the Bible talks about recompense or justice, it simply means that you and I will get what is right for us, what is coming to us.

Now, as blood-bought children of God, we know that as long as we trust in the Lord and are obedient to Him and repentant of our sins and failures, we will not get what's coming to us in the form of punishment for our sins, but we do get rewards for our righteousness. Jesus took our punishment, and we get His inheritance.

The Bible says in Psalm 37:1,2: **Fret not yourself because of evildoers, neither be envious against those who work unrighteousness (that which is not upright or in right standing with God). For they shall soon be cut down like the grass, and wither as the green herb.**

The love of God is shed abroad in our hearts by the Holy Spirit. (Rom. 5:5.) We don't want anyone to "be cut down" and "wither," even those who have harmed us. In my own life, I thank God I have come to the place of not wanting to see my tormentors have a miserable life. But what God has promised us who belong to Him and follow Him is that those who have hurt us will one day pay for their transgressions against us, unless they come to a place of repentance. But God will make it up to us if we trust Him to do so.

Too often believers don't seem to realize they are not to take matters into their own hands. Many of them are angry at what has been done to them — and that anger manifests itself in many destructive ways.

Part of the problem is that we as Christians have not yet learned that "into each life some rain must fall." Psalm 34:19 says, **Many evils confront the [consistently] righteous....** Even though we are the children of God not everything will go just the way we want, and not everyone will treat us just the way we would like to be treated.

But the Bible teaches that if we continue to trust God no matter what happens to us, if we keep our eyes on Him and have faith and confidence in Him, He will balance out the scales. The second half of Psalm 34:19 says, **...but the Lord delivers him out of them all!** The time will come when everything will be set straight. Our enemies will be repaid for all their treachery, and we will be paid back double for all we have lost and suffered.

True justice is worth waiting for.

A VERY GREAT RECOMPENSE

After these things, the word of the Lord came to Abram in a vision, saying, Fear not, Abram, I am your Shield, your abundant compensation, and your reward shall be exceedingly great. Genesis 15:1

In this passage we see that the Lord came to Abraham and promised that if he would be faithful and obedient to Him, He Himself would be his great recompense and reward. Later in Galatians 3 we are told that the blessing of Abraham was not just for him alone, but for all of us who are the children of Abraham through faith in God's Son Jesus Christ.

Each of us can be as blessed as Abraham was, if we will be as faithful and obedient as he was.

In our ministry, my husband and I have a fabulous life. God is so good to us! Many times things are so wonderful for us I feel like a fairy princess. I am amazed at what God has done as I think to myself, "Here I am traveling all over the world, people are coming to hear me speak, I'm on radio and television, and God is opening doors to me everywhere I go — I am so blessed!"

God will bless you too — if you will walk in His ways and trust Him to be your recompense, your very great reward, your vindicator. Before the blessings came, I had to learn to let go and let God handle the situations.

In Genesis 12:3, as part of the covenant the Lord made with Abraham, God told Abraham that if he would obey Him, God would bless those who blessed him and curse those who cursed him.

If you will stop being angry at all the things that have happened to you, and quit trying to get revenge on all those who have harmed you, the God of justice will balance it all out and make it all right!

For years I went around bemoaning my past and all the unfair things that had been done to me in my lifetime. For years I kept asking God, "Why me, Lord? Why me?" I was driving myself crazy with that self-pitying question.

Finally the Lord spoke to me and said, "Joyce, you can be pitiful or you can be powerful. Which do you want to be?"

All of us manifest what has happened to us in our life. Our past experiences are the cause of much of our negative attitude and behavior. But while it may be the reason we *are* the way we are, it is not any reason to *stay* that way.

God is telling each of us today, "If you will trust Me enough to turn over your past life to Me and let Me handle it, I will make it all up to you. Quit trying to do it yourself; you're only making things worse!"

One important part of leaving things in the hands of God involves forgiveness, which we will discuss in more detail later.

One man once told me, "I operate a counseling center, and the number one problem with the people we counsel is unforgiveness."

From my own life and ministry I know that is true. Although we have heard many messages on the subject of forgiveness, we still have to learn to deal with it. Otherwise the scales of justice in our lives will never be balanced, and we will never experience the full, abundant life God wants to bestow upon us.

If you will learn to trust all of your past to the Lord, He has promised to repay those who have caused you misery (although God's way of repaying is often different from the way we would imagine) and to repay you twofold for the misery you have suffered. Isn't it worth giving up all past hurts for that kind of a recompense and reward?

THE TWO WAYS

Enter through the narrow gate; for wide is the gate and spacious and broad is the way that leads away to destruction, and many are those who are entering through it.

But the gate is narrow (contracted by pressure) and the way is straitened and compressed that leads away to life, and few are those who find it. Matthew 7:13,14

We have seen that Jesus said, "I am the Way." Here in this passage, He speaks of two different ways: the broad way that leads to destruction and the narrow way that leads to life.

As I was meditating on this passage, the Lord quickened it to me by saying, "Joyce, on the broad way there is room for all kinds of fleshly things like bitterness and unforgiveness and resentment and vindictiveness. But on the narrow way there is only room for the Spirit."

In the flesh it is easy to take the broad path, but the end result is destruction. It is much harder to take the narrow path that leads to life.

Emotions move us to take the easy way, to do what feels good for the moment. Wisdom moves us to take the hard way that leads to life.

The question is: which will we choose?

GOD WANTS TO BE GOOD TO YOU!

> And therefore the Lord [earnestly] waits [expecting, looking, and longing] to be gracious to you; and therefore He lifts Himself up, that He may have mercy on you and show loving-kindness to you. For the Lord is a God of justice. Blessed (happy, fortunate, to be envied) are all those who [earnestly] wait for Him, who expect and look and long for Him [for His victory, His favor, His love, His peace, His joy, and His matchless, unbroken companionship]! Isaiah 30:18

Notice again that God is a God of justice! He waits and expects and looks and longs to do the right thing!

Hebrews 6:10 tells us, **For God is not unrighteous to forget or overlook your labor and the love which you have shown for His name's sake....** That's why all of us who earnestly wait for Him are blessed.

God is in His heaven waiting to be good to you and me. He is a God of mercy and justice, not of anger and punishment. He wants to balance out the scales of our lives, to make it up to us for all the hurts and wounds we have suffered — no matter what they may be.

Whatever your present situation or past experience, God wants to be good to you! He has a good plan for your life.

KEEP WALKING!

> And your ears will hear a word behind you, saying, This is the way; walk in it.... Isaiah 30:21

No matter what has happened to you in your lifetime, even if you have been abandoned by your spouse or abused by your parents or hurt by your children or others, if you will stay on that narrow path and leave all your excess baggage behind, sooner or later you will find the peace, joy, and fulfillment you seek.

Jesus is the Way, and He has shown us the way in which we are to walk. The Lord has sent upon us His Holy Spirit to lead and guide us in the way we are to go, the narrow way that leads to life and not the broad way that leads to destruction.

We must keep walking in the ways of the Lord: **And let us not lose heart and grow weary and faint in acting nobly and doing right, for in due time and at the appointed season we shall reap, if we do not loosen and relax our courage and faint** (Gal. 6:9).

The Bible does not promise that when we do right, we will reap the reward immediately. But it does assure us that if we keep doing right, eventually we will be rewarded.

God says, "As long as the earth remains, there will be seedtime and harvest." (Gen. 8:22, author's paraphrase.) We might read it like this, "As long as the earth remains, there will be SEED, TIME, and HARVEST." We must be patient like the farmer. He plants the seed and *expectantly* waits for the harvest. He looks forward to and talks about the harvest.

If you will continue to walk in the way the Lord has prescribed for you in His Word and by His Spirit — both in this life and in eternity — you will enjoy the recompense for *everything* you have suffered.

So keep walking the narrow path that leads to life — life in all its fullness and abundance!

3
HEALING OF DAMAGED EMOTIONS, PART 2
ᘓ

In this chapter we will look at the steps through which the Holy Spirit leads us in the healing of damaged emotions.

I first became aware of these steps when the Holy Spirit led me through them to healing from the damaged emotions I had suffered from years of abuse in my early life.

I believe they will help you too as you seek to find victory over your emotional problems and restoration of your broken spirit.

STEP 1: FACE THE TRUTH
ᘓ

> ...If you abide in My word [hold fast to My teachings and live in accordance with them], you are truly My disciples.
>
> And you will know the Truth, and the Truth will set you free. John 8:31,32

If you are to receive emotional healing, one of the first things you must learn to do is face the truth.

You cannot be set free while living in denial. You cannot pretend either that certain negative things did not happen to you, or that you have not been influenced by them or reacted in response to them.

Many times people who have suffered abuse or some other tragedy in their lives try to act as though it never happened.

For example, let's suppose a young girl has an abortion or bears a child out of wedlock and then gives it up for adoption. That traumatic experience can cause her to be emotionally damaged and wounded in later life because she develops opinions and attitudes about herself based on what she did.

In the same way, a person who has suffered through verbal, physical, or sexual abuse can develop a bad self-image under the misguided concept that if she was mistreated, there must have been something wrong with her to bring it on herself or that she must have deserved it.

From my own experience, as well as my years of ministry to others, I have come to realize that we human beings are marvelously adept at building walls and cramming things into dark corners, pretending they never happened.

During the eighteen years of my early life that I spent in an abusive environment, I had to face the fact of what was happening to me while it was actually taking place. But as soon as I got out into the world away from that situation, I acted as though nothing was wrong. I actually lived two separate lives at the same time. I never told anyone what was going on in my private life.

Why don't we want to bring things like that out into the open? We are afraid of what people will think. We are afraid of being rejected, of being misunderstood, of losing the love of those we care about who might have a different opinion of us if they really knew all about us.

It is so wonderful to have Jesus as a friend, because we don't have to hide anything from Him. He already knows everything about us anyway. We can always come to Him and know we will be loved and accepted no matter what we have suffered or how we have reacted to it.

We must remember that God knows *everything*. The Bible says He even knows the words in our mouth that are yet unuttered. (Ps. 139:1-4.)

One time in the early days of my walk with the Lord, before I learned I could not hide anything from Him, while I was praying I began to ponder whether I should tell Him something I had on my heart.

As I was debating within myself, God spoke to me and said, "Joyce, I already know all about it."

"Well, then, why do I have to tell You, if You already know?" I asked.

Do you know why we have to tell the Lord what is going on in our hearts and lives? He wants us to get it out in the open! That is part of the healing process.

If you are having problems in your life right now, whatever they may be, face the truth, then acknowledge it to the Lord in prayer. Ask the Holy Spirit to heal you, and He will begin to lead and guide you in the healing process.

STEP 2: CONFESS YOUR FAULTS

Confess to one another therefore your faults (your slips, your false steps, your offenses, your sins) and pray [also] for one another, that you may be healed and restored [to a spiritual tone of mind and heart]. The earnest (heartfelt, continued) prayer of a righteous man makes tremendous power available [dynamic in its working]. James 5:16

I think there is a place for eventually sharing with someone else that which has occurred in our life. There is something about verbalizing it to another person that does wonders for us.

But use wisdom. Be Spirit-led. Choose someone you know you can trust. Be sure that by sharing your burden with someone else, you do not place it upon that individual's shoulders. Also don't go on a digging expedition, trying to dig up old injuries long buried and forgotten.

For example, if you were abused by your grandfather forty years ago, and now your grandmother is eighty-five years old, don't decide to go to her and tell her what happened way back then. That would not be wise. It might help you to release it — but it would burden her.

It is so important to use wisdom and balance in these matters. If you are going to share your problems with someone, let God show you who to choose as a confidant. Pick a mature believer, someone who is not going to be burdened down or harmed by what you share or use it to hurt you or make you feel worse about yourself.

Many times there is a release that comes to us when we finally tell someone else those things that have been crammed in the background of our lives for years, especially when we discover that the person with whom we share them still loves and accepts us in spite of them.

When I finally worked up the courage to share with someone what had happened to me in my early life, I actually shook violently every time I tried to talk about it. I felt just like I had had a hard chill. It was an emotional reaction to the things I had kept buried within me for so long. I was shaking with fear.

Now when I talk about my past, it is as though I am talking about somebody else's problems. Because I have been healed and restored, my past doesn't bother me anymore. I know I am a new creature in Christ. (2 Cor. 5:17.)

Many times in my meetings, people will come to me to share things that happened to them twenty, thirty, or even forty or fifty years ago. Often they will weep and sob as the horrible truth comes out. I believe many of them get total release when they realize they can talk about these hurtful things and still be accepted.

I tell them, "God loves and accepts you, and I love and accept you. What happened to you in the past is not going to make any difference to your Christian friends."

STEP 3: ADMIT THE TRUTH TO YOURSELF

> Behold, You desire truth in the inner being;
> make me therefore to know wisdom in my inmost
> heart. Psalm 51:6

God wants us to face the truth in our inmost being, then confess it in an appropriate manner to the right person. Sometimes the person who needs to hear it most is us.

When people come to me for help in this area, I often tell them, "Go and look at yourself in the mirror and confess the problem to yourself."

Perhaps your problem is that your parents did not love you as a child.

"How could I ever verbalize that or say that to anybody else?" you may be asking. You can do it with the help of the Holy Spirit within you.

I believe that in order to go forward, we have to face facts. If it is true that your parents did not love you, you need to face that reality once and for all. You need to look at yourself in a mirror and say, "My parents did not love me, and what's more perhaps they never will love me."

Some people spend their entire lives trying to get something they will never have. If you have let the fact that you were unloved ruin your life thus far, don't let it ruin the rest of your life.

Do what David did in Psalm 27:10. Confess to yourself: **Although my father and my mother have forsaken me, yet the Lord will take me up [adopt me as His child].**

Whatever the problem may be that is bothering you, face it, consider confessing it to a trusted confidant, then admit it to yourself in your inmost being.

I heard of a doctor who intermittently in his life would leave his medical practice and become a bum on the street. When someone after many years finally got to the root of the doctor's problem, it was discovered that he had spent all of his life seeking words of approval and acceptance from his father who had always rejected him.

He had worked hard to become a doctor, thinking that would earn the approval and acceptance he sought. When it didn't, he worked even harder to build up a very successful practice, thinking surely then his father would be proud of him. He would go to see his father, sharing his achievements and accomplishments, only to experience more rejection.

When we try hard and fail, often we experience times of physical, mental, and emotional burnout. It was at such times that the doctor would go off the deep end emotionally and turn from his successful medical practice to the life of a homeless beggar.

As he faced the truth that his father had a problem and was

unable to show love, the doctor was restored to mental and emotional wholeness!

STEP 4: RECEIVE FORGIVENESS AND FORGET YOUR SIN

...For I will forgive their iniquity, and I will [seriously] remember their sin no more. Jeremiah 31:34

No matter what your problem or how bad you feel about yourself as a result of it, God loves you. In Jesus Christ He has given you a new life. He has given you a new family and new friends to love and accept and appreciate and support you. You are okay, and you are going to make it because of the One Who lives on the inside of you and cares for you.

You may have to look at yourself in the mirror and confess, "I had an abortion. I did that, Lord, and it is a marvel to me to realize that I can stand here and look myself in the eye. But I can do so because I know that, even though I did that horrible thing that is so wrong, You have put my sins as far away from me as the east is from the west, and You remember them no more!"

No matter what we may have done, we need to get a deeper revelation of what God means when He says, "I will remember your sins no more."

Once we have confessed our sins and asked for God's forgiveness, if we continue to drag them up to Him every time we go to Him in prayer, we are reminding Him of something He has promised to forget, something He has removed from us as far as the east is from the west. (Ps. 103:12.)

Once you have confessed your sins to God and asked Him to forgive you of them, He has not only *forgiven* them, but He has actually *forgotten* them.

You need to do the same. Stop punishing yourself for something that no longer exists.

STEP 5: ACKNOWLEDGE YOURSELF AS A NEW CREATURE

> Therefore if any person is [ingrafted] in Christ (the Messiah) he is a new creation (a new creature altogether); the old [previous moral and spiritual condition] has passed away. Behold, the fresh and new has come! 2 Corinthians 5:17

In my past I did many things that I am not proud of. For example, when I was a child, I was a regular thief. I would steal anything I could get my hands on. That is terrible, but of course I don't steal now and so I don't make myself miserable about what I used to do as a child. I believe I stole things because I was being abused, and stealing made me feel I was in control of something in my life instead of always being controlled by everything and everybody.

There was also a time in my life when I was a bar maid. Now I am serving New Wine, so I don't worry about what I used to do in the past.

You see, it is a tremendous testimony to be able to admit what we were, but to testify to the fact that our old man — the old person we were — has died and we are a brand new person in Christ.

The Bible tells us that our old man died and was buried and is now resurrected to new life, so that you and I are now seated in heavenly places in Christ Jesus. (Eph. 2:5,6.)

Why then should I be ashamed to admit to something that happened in my old life? It is no problem for me to talk about a dead person!

If you and I are new creatures in Christ Jesus and old things have passed away, we need to forget about them!

No matter what happened to you in the past or what was done to you, you should feel free to look at anybody and say: "This is what I was, and this is what I did, but thank God, now I am a new creature in Christ Jesus. That is not me any more! You would not believe what God has done in my life!"

Remember what I said previously: "Bringing things out in the open causes them to lose their grip on us."

STEP 6: ASSUME PERSONAL RESPONSIBILITY

If we [freely] admit that we have sinned and confess our sins, He is faithful and just (true to His own nature and promises) and will forgive our sins [dismiss our lawlessness] and [continuously] cleanse us from all unrighteousness [everything not in conformity to His will in purpose, thought, and action].

If we say (claim) we have not sinned, we contradict His Word and make Him out to be false and a liar, and His Word is not in us [the divine message of the Gospel is not in our hearts].

1 John 1:9,10

Some people are trapped in denial, afraid of what might happen if others found out the truth about them. But as long as they deny the past, they are never going to be set free from it.

Nobody can be set free from a problem until he is willing to admit he has a problem. An alcoholic or a drug addict or anyone who has lost control of his life is doomed to suffer until he is able to say, "I've got a problem, and I need help with it."

Rather than facing responsibility for our own problems, we generally want to blame others. Unwillingness to face and accept personal responsibility is childish.

I have learned a lot from our youngest son. He is so sweet, and I am so glad that God gave him to us. He keeps me young and on my toes.

Although Danny is now born again and Spirit-filled, as a child he walked totally in the flesh. One evidence is the fact that he never wanted to take responsibility for anything he did wrong. No matter what happened, it was never Danny's fault.

One time I was in the van with him and looked back to see how he was doing. The entire back end of that vehicle was strewn with litter: potato chip crumbs and sacks, a crushed Coke can, and the like. I said, "Danny, for crying out loud, clean up that mess back there!"

"It's not my fault!" he cried.

"Whose fault is it then?" I asked. "I'm not back there!"

"Well, Dad gave me the can and the chips!" he explained.

Although he had taken what had been handed to him and had strewn it everywhere, it wasn't his fault. It was his father's fault for having given it to him. He was thus able to shift responsibility from himself to someone else.

We all do exactly the same thing in our lives!

A while back, I had gained some weight but hadn't realized it. When I got dressed, I would complain to my husband about the lady who helped me with my laundry.

"What is she doing to my clothes?" I would ask. "She is ruining them by shrinking them! I told her not to put them in the dryer but to send them to the cleaners!"

If it was an article of clothing that had been sent to the cleaners, I would say, "What are those people doing to my clothes, shrinking them like this!" I was laying the blame for my ill-fitting garments on someone else!

I continued on like this until the day I stepped on a scale and saw my weight had gone up six or seven pounds. Suddenly it hit me. It wasn't my clothes that were getting smaller, it was me who was getting bigger!

I had to say to myself, "Joyce, you have gained weight, and you have gained it because you have been eating too much!"

Just as I had to face the truth and accept responsibility for my own actions in that situation, each of us must face the truth about ourselves and assume the responsibility for our problems and their solution.

Even though our problems may have been brought upon us because of something done to us against our will, we have no excuse for allowing them to persist or even to grow and take control over our entire life. Our past experiences may have made us the way we are, but we don't have to stay that way. We can take the initiative and start doing something to change things.

STEP 7: FOLLOW THE SPIRIT OF TRUTH

But when He, the Spirit of Truth (the Truth-
giving Spirit) comes, He will guide you into all the
Truth (the whole, full Truth).... John 16:13

As we have seen, to be healed, we must face the truth and acknowledge the situation in which we find ourselves. We must stop trying to blame someone else for everything wrong with us. Trying to blame the way we are now on what happened to us earlier in life is not even healthy.

I used to have a hard time getting along with people, and I was sure it was because of the way I had been treated in my younger days. But once I began to ask the Lord to heal me, He began to reveal to me the truth about myself and my situation.

One of the things He revealed to me was that every time the Holy Spirit tried to guide me into some unpleasant truth about myself, my immediate reaction would always be to say, "Yes, *but...*"

The Lord showed me that an excuse just covers up the root of the problem so that it is never exposed, and the person is never able to be set free.

When someone corrects you, do you do what I used to do and make an excuse, or do you face the truth and admit you are wrong? Admitting we are wrong is one of the hardest things we ever do in life.

One time my husband came home late from playing golf after he had promised to be back in time for dinner. By the time he arrived I had prepared my speech in great detail. I immediately laid into him, telling him if he was going to be late, he should call and let me know. I was really getting ready to unload on him when he looked at me and said, "You are absolutely right." It just blew my whole case. Then he went on to say, "I'll pray and ask God to help me not do it again." There was nothing left for me to say. His speaking truth prevented a major argument.

Yet many times when God tries to tell us something we are doing wrong, we find it so hard to simply say, "Lord, You are absolutely right. I have no excuse. I ask You to forgive me and help me to overcome this fault."

I believe that kind of honesty in our relationship with God and other people stops the devil from running rampant in our lives. I don't think Satan knows what to do with that kind of truth, any more than I did when Dave spoke it to me. Truth puts an end to the devil's reign.

INNER HEALING VERSUS EMOTIONAL HEALING

...I will ask the Father, and He will give you another Comforter (Counselor, Helper, Intercessor, Advocate, Strengthener, and Standby), that He may remain with you forever —

The Spirit of Truth, Whom the world cannot receive (welcome, take to its heart), because it does not see Him or know and recognize Him. But you know and recognize Him, for He lives with you [constantly] and will be in you. John 14:16,17

In John 16:13 Jesus called the Holy Spirit "the Spirit of Truth." Here in this passage, He tells us this Spirit has been sent to live within each of us. If the Spirit of Truth is in us, what is His primary function? According to Jesus, it is to guide us into all truth.

A teaching within the Church which I feel I need to caution you about, although many believers will disagree with my viewpoint, is called "inner healing."

I am all in favor of inner healing, but I prefer to call it "emotional healing," to distinguish it from what is being taught and practiced in some Christian circles today.

I believe the motive behind the inner healing message is right. Those who teach and practice it just want to help people, but I sincerely believe some of their techniques are dangerous.

Inner healing is a method used in healing hurts of the past. It is often quite effective, but we must realize that even ungodly methods sometimes work.

Let me give you an example. A friend of mine was involved in transcendental meditation when she was saved. She went to her pastor to ask him about it, and he said he had no problem with it, adding, "If it works, let me know."

This woman was seeking peace, and so she was open to whatever was effective in helping her find it. As she got further into this movement, she learned that it involves Eastern-style meditation and repeating a *mantra*, which Webster defines as "a mystical formula of invocation or incantation (as in Hinduism)."[1]

As she and the other participants sat and meditated, repeating this invocation or incantation, they began to move into a trance-like state. Eventually, they were supposed to progress to the point where mystical beings or "spirit guides" appeared and began to lead and instruct them.

Since she was now saved, my friend thought if this method was spiritually sound, it would still be effective if she replaced her mantra with the name of Jesus. So she went into her trancelike state and began to repeat the name of Jesus. Suddenly a spirit knocked her from one side of the room to the other, and she knew right then that something was very wrong! She quickly got out of that movement and went back into her local Christian church. She was sincerely right in her search for help, sincerely wrong in her choice of method.

Another friend had something of the same kind of experience while experimenting with a popular mind-control system.

All such methods of so-called inner healing or inner enlightenment are outside of the Church of Jesus Christ and should be avoided.

"Why?" you may ask. "What could be wrong with visualizing healing, comfort, forgiveness, and restoration?"

Yes, it does *sound* good. It seems as if it would be within the realm of the Church. That's why so many desperate people are getting involved in it. They don't really stop to ask themselves, "Does it line up with Scripture?" The fact is that no such system or method can be found anywhere in the Word of God.

The main thing I see wrong with it is the major role that visualization or imagination plays in it. As Christians, Jesus should always play the primary role in everything we do, not mystical occultic figures out of the imagination.

Another thing I find wrong with this type of inner healing is the fact that the person and not the Holy Spirit is the initiator. In some of these methods, the individual is supposed to get into a meditative state, clear his mind, and begin visualizing going back in time to the moment of the wounding of his emotions.

Sometimes these rearward progressions go all the way back to the womb or to the time of birth. The participant is told to reenact the scene of his emotional wounding in his mind, visualizing Jesus coming in and bringing healing to that traumatic event.

The only problem is that, in my opinion, the Jesus who comes on the scene in such cases is just a figment of the person's imagination and not the real Jesus of the Bible.

I recently read the life story of a man who thought Jesus was appearing to him. He experienced three visions of what he believed to be Jesus. The figure he saw in these visions was surrounded by a great light which produced in him a temporary sense of peace and well-being. Then the figure began to speak to him and give him directions and instructions.

One of the things this man was actually *forced* to do was go down to the beach and witness to others. The voice made it clear this was something he had to do whether he wanted to or not — and right away!

If this man had known the Word of God, he would have realized then and there what he was encountering was not God. God does not force His children to do anything. He leads and guides by His Holy Spirit, but it is always in a sweet and gentle manner. No one is ever required to do anything under duress, as though his salvation depended on it!

HEALING OR DECEPTION?

I have received tremendous healing from the Lord Jesus Christ. But in order to receive that healing I did not have to go through any of the methods or techniques prescribed and practiced in the popular inner healing movement. I just allowed the Holy Spirit to lead and guide me.

If you pray and ask God to help you by bringing you into a place of emotional healing, He will lead and guide you Himself. He has an individualized plan for each one of us, and it will always line up with Scripture.

For example, some years ago I was praying for God to heal my troubled life. While I was in this period of prayer, a woman came into our church and gave her testimony. Her background and experience were almost identical to mine. My husband recognized it and advised me to buy the book she had written on the subject.

I bought the book and started reading it. In it this woman, who is now in ministry, began to reenact some of the events that had taken place in her life. All of a sudden I started having flashbacks. I realized it was the Holy Spirit Who was bringing those scenes to my memory to help me deal with them and receive healing from them.

That is the way true emotional healing works. It is initiated by the Holy Spirit, not by anything that is conjured up by the one seeking help.

If you are in need of emotional healing, don't try to conjure up something that makes you feel better. Go to the Lord and ask Him to lead and guide you by His Holy Spirit in the ways you should go. Then be ready to face whatever He wants you to confront to bring about your full restoration.

Don't allow anyone to influence you into going back and digging up things from your past that you may not be prepared to face yet. It can be devastating!

One of the sweet things about the Holy Spirit is the fact that He leads us one step at a time. He knows when we are ready and able to face certain things. When God Himself brings us face to face with certain harsh realities in our lives, we can know that it is the right time to deal with those painful issues.

Remember, spiritual revelation comes from God, not from man.

Beware of so-called spirit guides. Satan tries to pervert the work of the Holy Spirit by offering deceptive imitations to lead people away from true spiritual encounters. Be very careful about who and what you follow. Pray and ask the Lord to keep you from deception.

There is a lot of spiritual "junk" being offered today, and some of it sounds so good and feels so right. Make sure what you are following is in line with the Word of God and is initiated by His Holy Spirit. When you open up your spirit for guidance and direction, make sure you are opening it up to the Spirit of God, not an imitator.

Opening Up to God
ی

> And this is the message [the message of promise] which we have heard from Him and now are reporting to you: God is Light, and there is no darkness in Him at all [no, not in any way].
>
> [So] if we say we are partakers together and enjoy fellowship with Him when we live and move and are walking about in darkness, we are [both] speaking falsely and do not live and practice the Truth [which the Gospel presents]. 1 John 1:5,6

This is a great Scripture passage because it shows us that if we will take responsibility for ourselves and our own situation, and not try to blame someone else, it will be the first step toward receiving our healing.

So often the things we try to hide by burying them deep inside ourselves become darkness within us. But this passage tells us in God there is no darkness at all. So when we allow Him full entrance into our hearts and minds, there will be no darkness there.

I am so glad that God fills every room in my heart, so that I am filled with His light. There are no places in my heart that I know of that are blocked off from Him and the light that comes with His presence.

Often one of the signs that we are walking in the light of the Gospel is that we have good relationships with everyone with whom we come in contact in our daily lives — including our spouse and our children.

I can truthfully say that right now I do not know of any person in my life with whom I have a major problem. And it is not because *they* have all changed. The reason is that I have allowed the Lord to come into those dark recesses of my heart and fill them with His marvelous light. I have opened up myself to the searching, cleansing light of the Holy Spirit of God. The result is that while I used to live and walk in darkness and fear and misery, now I live and walk in light and peace and joy.

When I was one person on the inside and another person on the outside, I had to wear masks and be phony. I had to put on a facade and play games. I am so glad that now I can stand before God and my family and everyone else and be at peace with myself and with others.

I no longer have to live in fear of what anyone thinks of me, because I have opened my heart to God's Holy Spirit, and He has lighted up the dark places within me so I can live free!

You can say the same thing if you will open your heart to God and allow Him to fill every part of you with His life-giving Spirit.

THE NOSE KNOWS!

But if we [really] are living and walking in the Light, as He [Himself] is in the Light, we have [true, unbroken] fellowship with one another, and the blood of Jesus Christ His Son cleanses (removes) us from all sin and guilt [keeps us cleansed from sin in all its forms and manifestations]. 1 John 1:7

I like the last part of this verse which speaks of the blood of Jesus cleansing us from sin and all of its forms and manifestations.

Let me give you an example of how this works in our everyday lives.

If there is something rotten in your refrigerator, you will know it is there every time you open the door because you will smell it. You may not know what it is or exactly where it is located, but you can be sure that it is in there somewhere.

I believe our lives are like that. If there is something rotten within us, those who come in close contact with us are going to perceive it, whether they know what it is or why it is there. They will "smell" it, or sense it.

In 2 Corinthians 2:15 the Apostle Paul tells us that as believers ...**we are the sweet fragrance of Christ [which exhales] unto God, [discernible alike] among those who are being saved and among those who are perishing**.

Unfortunately, it also works in the opposite way. When there is something within us that has been shut away and become rotten and spoiled, it gives off a totally different aroma, detectable by everyone.

That's why we must open up ourselves and allow the Holy Spirit to come in and cleanse our hearts and remove whatever is causing us to give off a foul stench.

When we open ourselves to the Lord and let Him begin to cleanse and heal us from within, we will find ourselves coming into better and better fellowship with all those around us. It won't happen overnight, because it is a process. But it will begin to take place, one step at a time.

GETTING AT THE ROOT OF THE PROBLEM

If we say we have so sin [refusing to admit that
we are sinners], we delude and lead ourselves astray,

and the Truth [which the Gospel presents] is not in us [does not dwell in our hearts].

If we [freely] admit that we have sinned and confess our sins, He is faithful and just (true to His own nature and promises) and will forgive our sins [dismiss our lawlessness] and [continuously] cleanse us from all unrighteousness [everything not in conformity to His will in purpose, thought, and action]. 1 John 1:8,9

In this passage, we see that we can never expect to find a solution to our sin problem until we are willing to admit we have a sin problem, then allow the Lord to cleanse us of it. Part of that process involves taking a spiritual inventory of ourselves to get at the root cause of our sin.

When you are having emotional problems, one of the things I encourage you to do is to realize the emotions you are experiencing are not the problem, but only its manifestation. What you need to do is not just deal with the symptoms, your emotions, but to get at the root of the problem, whatever it is that is causing you to feel the way you do.

Generally we pay far too much attention to our feelings. We say things like: "I *feel* that nobody cares for me," "I *feel* that others don't love or understand me," "I *feel* that people don't pay enough attention to me."

Those thoughts and statements are evidence that we are being influenced by what we perceive from our emotions rather than what is actually taking place in our lives.

Let me give you an example.

Let's say that a woman feels that her husband does not pay her enough attention. So she prays and asks God to make her husband more attentive to her. When her prayer isn't answered, she sets in to make it happen herself. She gripes and complains to her husband, "You're not paying enough attention to me; you don't care anything about me or my feelings."

The truth is that no matter how much attention her husband or anyone else pays to her, she will never be satisfied. It will never be enough. Why? Because she is trying to get from other people what can only come from God. She is trying to build her self-image on the feedback and opinions of others rather than on her own worth in the eyes of the Lord.

Her problem may seem to be that she is not loved and appreciated, but the root of the problem is the fact that she *feels* that way because she was starved emotionally as a child. As a result, now that she is an adult she demands more from others than they are prepared or able to give. So she smothers everyone who comes into relationship with her. If she doesn't realize what is happening and do something about it, she will end up having no relationships at all.

Unless she gets at the root of the problem and solves it, she will go through her whole life blaming others, claiming her problem is their fault because they are not sensitive to her or appreciative of her.

She is listening to her feelings and emotions rather than getting at the root of the problem and discovering what is really causing her to feel the way she does.

Here is another example from my own life. When I was having so many emotional problems, I used to explode and throw a fit if things didn't go just the way I wanted them to.

I could be working in the kitchen peacefully and calmly, but if my kids came through the back door and let it slam, "BOOM!" I would become a totally different person. I would get upset and jump all over them.

Then I would go to the Lord in prayer and say, "God, what's wrong with me?" Since I was sure there was nothing wrong with me, what I was really asking was, "What's wrong with these people?"

I was thoroughly convinced that if others didn't do what they did, then I wouldn't react the way I did.

But the truth is, I was the one who was at fault.

If one of my children came through the door and tripped on the threshold and fell down, instead of saying, "Oh, honey, are you all right?" I would lash out and yell, "What's the matter with you! Can't you even come in the house without making a mess? For crying out loud, do I have to teach you how to walk?"

I was continually blaming my feelings on someone or something else. But one day in the midst of my prayer, "God, what's wrong with me?" He showed me what it was — and it was a life-changing revelation to me.

The Lord spoke to me and said, "You go through life doing all the things you think you are supposed to do to be a good wife and mother and Christian, but the truth is that inside you feel guilty and condemned about everything — from not praying enough to feeling responsible for the things that happened to you in your past."

Then He went on to say, "Those feelings put pressure on you which builds up inside. Because you are at home most of the time by yourself, you have no one to vent your emotions on, so you become like a pressure cooker. The first time something happens to overload your system, you explode."

That may be what is happening with you. Like me, you may have so much pressure building up inside you because of your unresolved feelings and emotions that whenever anything happens you don't like, it "sets you off." Like me, you may not even know what is causing you to react the way you do.

I have read that medical studies indicate 75 percent of physical sickness is caused by emotional problems.[2] And one of the greatest emotional problems people experience is guilt. Many people are punishing themselves with sickness. They are refusing to relax and enjoy life because, after all, they don't *deserve* to have a good time. So they live in the perpetual penance of regret and remorse. This kind of stress makes people sick.

If that describes you, the only answer is to call upon the Holy Spirit to help you get at the root of the problem that is causing you so much misery. Only He knows what to do to help you.

I am reminded of a little story I heard about Henry Ford. One day some piece of important equipment in his automobile factory was not working right so he called a friend named Steinmetz, who was a real mechanical genius. His body was deformed, but his mind was phenomenal.

When Ford saw that nobody else could repair the piece of badly needed machinery, Ford called in Steinmetz who fiddled around with it for about ten minutes and had it working again. The two friends rejoiced, and Steinmetz left.

A few days later Ford received a bill from Steinmetz for ten thousand dollars! He immediately called up his friend and complained, "Don't you think this is a little steep? Ten thousand dollars is a lot of money to pay someone for tinkering around for ten minutes."

Steinmetz calmly answered, "Well, ten dollars of that bill was for the ten minutes I spent tinkering; $9,990 was for knowing where to tinker."

The reason the Holy Spirit is so valuable in this type of healing is because He knows where to tinker!

The Holy Spirit is the only One Who knows you better than you know yourself. He knows what is wrong with you and what to do about it. The best thing you can do to solve your problem is to call Him on the job and let Him do the "tinkering" that is needed. As He does so, be patient. Remember: emotional healing is a process, one that takes time.

PITIFUL OR POWERFUL?

> Be well balanced (temperate, sober of mind), be vigilant and cautious at all times; for that enemy of yours, the devil, roams around like a lion roaring [in fierce hunger], seeking someone to seize upon and devour.
>
> Withstand him; be firm in faith [against his onset — rooted, established, strong, immovable, and determined], knowing that the same (identical) sufferings are appointed to your brotherhood (the whole body of Christians) throughout the world. 1 Peter 5:8,9

If you want to receive emotional healing and go forward with your life, you must lay down self-pity. I am so convinced of that truth that I will go so far as to ask you the same question that God asked me several years ago: "Do you want to be pitiful or powerful?"

I will also pose some other questions for you on this same subject. The first one is: "Do you feel sorry for yourself?"

Be honest in your response. Don't do as I used to do and answer, "Yes, *but...*"

God has shown me that self-pity is like a wall that keeps us from going forward in life. In my own life, I had to learn that everyone has problems. Just because I was abused as a child, I am not a special case. Like everyone else, I have to take responsibility for my own healing and restoration — and so do you. We must cooperate with the work of the Holy Spirit in our lives.

My next question is: "Do you have a chip on your shoulder?"

For years I walked around with a huge chip on my shoulder because "what happened to me was not fair; it shouldn't have happened to a dog, so I *deserve...*"

It is a little hard on the flesh to have to admit that our special problems do not make us special cases. We are all special to God, but everybody has been hurt or abused in one way or another. Each of us has to take responsibility for our own behavior and avoid blaming the past or those who have hurt us.

The Bible tells us that those who wallow in self-pity make themselves vulnerable to the devil, who is seeking someone to devour.

If we don't want the devil to devour us, then we need to resist self-pity, blaming others, and carrying a chip on our shoulder. If we do things God's way, we will experience God's victory.

That's the message that the Lord was trying to get across to me when He asked me whether I wanted to be pitiful or powerful. He was saying to me then, just as He is saying to you now, "You may have a reason to feel sorry for yourself, but you have no right to do so, because I am willing to heal your life. I will deliver you from everything Satan has tried to do to you, and I will use it for your good and My glory."

All the hurts and wounds you have suffered, even the things you have done to wrong yourself, the Lord can make into the tools and equipment you need to minister to other hurting people.

THE WOUNDED HEALER
~

Blessed be the God and Father of our Lord Jesus Christ, the Father of sympathy (pity and mercy) and the God [Who is the Source] of every comfort (consolation and encouragement),

Who comforts (consoles and encourages) us in every trouble (calamity and affliction), so that we may also be able to comfort (console and encourage) those who are in any kind of trouble or distress, with the comfort (consolation and encouragement) with which we ourselves are comforted (consoled and encouraged) by God.
2 Corinthians 1:3,4

The best healer is often the wounded healer, because he knows what he is dealing with since he has suffered it himself. That's what Paul was saying in this passage from his letter to the church in Corinth.

If you have suffered through some hard times in your life, you are going to be even more successful in ministering to those who are going through the same kind of suffering in their lives.

That doesn't mean that those who have never suffered hardship or pain cannot be used by the Lord. Some of the greatest and most powerful ministers I know have lived almost perfect lives. But just because you and I have suffered does not keep us from ministering successfully also.

I am writing this book to help you realize that even though you may have had a rough time in your life, God can use what you have been through for His glory — if you will allow Him to do so!

If I were still back where I started out, feeling sorry for myself, I would be no good to myself or anyone else. In fact, I would probably be on the devil's lunch plate! He would be chewing me up and spitting me out. But because the Lord gave me the grace to lay down my self-pity and take up the challenge of living for Him, now I am able to help hundreds of thousands of people all over the nation and beyond.

To me the greatest testimony in the world is to be able to say, "God took what Satan tried to use to destroy me, and He turned it around for His glory and used it for the betterment of other people in the Kingdom."

It takes God to do that!

No matter where you may be today or what you may be going through, God can turn your situation around and use it to further His Kingdom and bring blessings to you and to many others.

COMPASSION OR PITY?

Now the doings (practices) of the flesh are clear (obvious): they are immorality, impurity, indecency,
Idolatry, sorcery, enmity, strife, jealousy, anger (ill temper), selfishness, divisions (dissensions), party spirit (factions, sects with peculiar opinions, heresies),
Envy, drunkenness, carousing, and the like....
Galatians 5:19-21

In the Bible the word "pity" always means compassion, which moves a person to action on behalf of someone else.

Pity or compassion is never used in the Scriptures to refer to feeling sorry for ourselves because of what we are going through. In fact, in that sense, self-pity is viewed as one of the sins of the flesh listed here in Galatians 5:19-21.

When the Lord first revealed that fact to me, I looked it up to be sure I had heard it correctly. But I couldn't find it there so I tried another translation. When I still couldn't find it, the Lord spoke to me and said, "It's called idolatry."

That's true. When we turn inward upon ourselves and begin to weep in pity for ourselves, what are we doing? We are idolizing ourselves. We are making ourselves the center of everything and feeling sorry for ourselves because everything in God's creation is not going the way we want it to.

Real pity or compassion moves us to action on behalf of someone else, but self-pity or idolatry drags us down into depression and hopelessness.

Do you recall what Paul and Silas did when they found themselves imprisoned in chains in the Philippian jail for trying to do good to others? Instead of feeling sorry for themselves, they began to sing and praise and rejoice in the Lord. As a result, they brought the jailer to repentance and salvation.

When faced with trials and problems, we have a choice. We can feel sorry for ourselves or we can lift our heads and look to the Lord to lead us out to victory, just as He did for Paul and Silas.

The choice is ours.

GET ON WITH LIFE
༈

David therefore besought God for the child; and
David fasted and went in and lay all night
[repeatedly] on the floor.

His older house servants arose [in the night] and went to him to raise him up from the floor, but he would not, nor did he eat food with them.

And on the seventh day the child died. David's servants feared to tell him that the child was dead, for they said, While the child was yet alive, we spoke to him and he would not listen to our voices; will he then harm himself if we tell him the child is dead?

But when David saw that his servants whispered, he perceived that the child was dead. So he said to them, Is the child dead? And they said, He is.

Then David arose from the floor, washed, anointed himself, changed his apparel, and went into the house of the Lord and worshiped. Then he came to his own house, and when he asked, they set food before him, and he ate.

Then his servants said to him, What is this that you have done? You fasted and wept while the child was alive, but when the child was dead, you arose and ate food.

David said, While the child was still alive, I fasted and wept; for I said, Who knows whether the Lord will be gracious to me and let the child live?

But now he is dead; why should I fast? Can I bring him back again? I shall go to him, but he will not return to me. 2 Samuel 12:16-23

What was David saying here in this passage? He was saying: "When my child was sick, I did everything I could to save him. Now that he is dead, there is nothing more I can do. Why should I sit around mourning over something I cannot change? It is much better for me if I get up and get on with my life."

That is what the Lord is encouraging us to do today. He is telling us to stop mourning over what has happened in the past and to make a decision that we are going to live today and every day for the rest of our lives. He is telling us not to ruin the time we have left grieving over what has been lost.

Now, obviously when experiencing the loss of a loved one there is a normal period of grieving that must be gone through — but if that grief period is allowed to go on too long it becomes destructive.

Make a vow right now that from this moment on you are not going to waste any more of your valuable time feeling sorry for yourself and wallowing in self-pity over things you cannot change. Instead pledge that you are going to live each day to the fullest, looking forward to what God has in store for you as you follow Him — one step at a time.

4
EMOTIONS AND THE PROCESS
OF FORGIVENESS

There are two things that cause us to get all knotted up inside. The first is the negative things done to us by others. The second is the negative things we have done to ourselves and others. We have a hard time getting over what others have done to us, and we find it difficult to forget what we have done to ourselves and others.

We have been examining how our emotions function because anything that destroys our confidence in ourselves or in others will affect not only us personally but also our relationships with other people.

In this chapter we are going to consider what we can expect from our emotions once we begin to learn to operate in forgiveness: of ourselves, of others, and of God.

BE QUICK TO FORGIVE

Let all bitterness and indignation and wrath (passion, rage, bad temper) and resentment (anger, animosity) and quarreling (brawling, clamor, contention) and slander (evil-speaking, abusive or

> blasphemous language) be banished from you, with
> all malice (spite, ill will, or baseness of any kind).
> And become useful and helpful and kind to one
> another, tenderhearted (compassionate, under-
> standing, loving-hearted), forgiving one another
> [*readily and freely*], as God in Christ forgave you.
> Ephesians 4:31,32

The Bible teaches us to forgive "readily and freely." We are to be quick to forgive.

According to 1 Peter 5:5 we are to clothe ourselves with the character of Jesus Christ, meaning that we are to be longsuffering, patient, not easily offended, slow to anger, quick to forgive, and filled with mercy.

My definition of the word "mercy" is the ability to look beyond what is done to discover the reason why it was done. Many times people do things even they don't understand themselves, but there is always a reason why people behave as they do.

The same is true of us as believers. We are to be merciful and forgiving, just as God in Christ forgives us our wrongdoing — even when we don't understand why we do what we do.

FORGIVE TO KEEP SATAN FROM TAKING ADVANTAGE

> If you forgive anyone anything, I too forgive that
> one; and what I have forgiven, if I have forgiven
> anything, has been for your sakes in the presence
> [and with the approval] of Christ (the Messiah),
> To keep Satan from getting the advantage over
> us; for we are not ignorant of his wiles and
> intentions. 2 Corinthians 2:10,11

The Bible teaches that we are to forgive in order **to keep Satan from getting the advantage over us.** So when we forgive others, not only are we doing them a favor, we are doing ourselves an even greater favor.

The reason we are doing ourselves such a favor is because unforgiveness produces in us a root of bitterness that poisons our entire system.

FORGIVENESS AND THE ROOT OF BITTERNESS

Exercise foresight and be on the watch to look [after one another], to see that no one falls back from and fails to secure God's grace (His unmerited favor and spiritual blessing), in order that no root of resentment (rancor, bitterness, or hatred) shoots forth and causes trouble and bitter torment, and the many become contaminated and defiled by it. Hebrews 12:15

When we are filled with unforgiveness, we are filled with resentment and bitterness.

The word *bitterness* is used to refer to something that is pungent or sharp to the taste.[1]

We remember that when the Children of Israel were about to be led out of Egypt, they were told by the Lord on the eve of their departure to prepare a Passover meal which included bitter herbs. Why? God wanted them to eat those bitter herbs as a reminder of the bitterness they had experienced in bondage.

Bitterness always belongs to bondage!

It is said that the bitter herbs the Israelites ate were probably akin to horseradish. If you have ever taken a big bite of horseradish, you know it can cause quite a physical reaction. Bitterness causes precisely the same type of reaction in us spiritually. Not only does it cause *us* discomfort, but it also causes discomfort to the Holy Spirit Who abides within us.

We have seen that we are to be a sweet-smelling fragrance to those who come in contact with us. But when we are filled with bitterness, the aroma we give off is not sweet but bitter.

How does bitterness get started? According to the Bible, it grows from a root. The *King James Version* of this verse speaks of a **root of bitterness.** A root of bitterness always produces the fruit of bitterness.

What is the seed from which that root sprouts? Unforgiveness.

Bitterness results from the many minor offenses we just won't let go of, the things we rehearse over and over inside of us until they become blown all out of proportion and grow to monumental size.

Besides all the little things we allow to get out of hand, there are the major offenses people commit or have committed against us. The longer we allow them to grow and fester, the more powerful they become, and the more they infect our entire being: our personality, our attitude and behavior, our perspective, and our relationships — especially our relationship with God.

LET IT GO!

And you shall hallow the fiftieth year and proclaim liberty throughout all the land to all its inhabitants. It shall be a jubilee for you....

And if your brother becomes poor beside you and sells himself to you, you shall not compel him to serve as a bondsman (a slave not eligible for redemption),

> But as a hired servant and as a temporary resident he shall be with you; he shall serve you till the Year of Jubilee,
>
> And then he shall depart from you, he and his children with him, and shall go back to his own family and return to the possession of his fathers.
> Leviticus 25:10,39-41

To keep Satan from getting the advantage over you, forgive! Do yourself a favor and let the offense go! Forgive to keep yourself from being poisoned — and imprisoned.

According to Webster, the word *forgive* means "to excuse for a fault or offense: PARDON."[2]

When a person is found guilty of a crime and sentenced to serve a prison term, we say that he owes a debt to society. But if he is pardoned, he is allowed to go his way freely with no restraints upon him. Such a pardon cannot be earned, it must be granted by a higher authority.

When someone has offended us, you and I tend to think that person owes us.

For example, a young woman once came through the prayer line in one of our meetings and told me she had just caught her husband cheating on her. Her reponse was, "He *owes* me!"

When someone has hurt us, we react just as if that individual had stolen something from us or wounded us physically. We feel that person owes us something. That's why Jesus taught us to pray in the Lord's Prayer, ...**Forgive us our debts, as we forgive our debtors** (Matt. 6:12).

In Leviticus 25 we read about the Year of Jubilee in which all debts were forgiven and all debtors were pardoned and set free.

When we are in Christ, every day can be the Year of Jubilee. We can say to those who are in debt to us by their mistreatment of us, "I forgive you and release you from your debt. You are free to go. I leave you in God's hands to let Him deal with you, because as long as I am trying to deal with you, He won't."

According to the Bible, we are not to hold people in perpetual debt, just as we ourselves are not to be indebted to anyone else: **Keep out of debt and owe no man anything, except to love one another...** (Rom. 13:8). We need to learn to pardon people, to cancel their debts to us.

Can you imagine the joy of a person who learns that he has been pardoned from a ten- or twenty-year prison sentence? That's the good news of the Cross. Because Jesus paid our debt for us, God can say to us, "You don't owe Me anything anymore!"

There is a song that conveys that thought with the words, "I owed a debt I could not pay; He paid a debt He did not owe."

Our trouble is either we are still trying to pay our debt to the Lord, or else we are still trying to collect our debts from others. Just as God canceled our debt and forgave us of it, so we are to cancel the debts of others and forgive them what they owe us.

LET IT DROP!
ॐ

> And whenever you stand praying, if you have anything against anyone, forgive him and let it drop (leave it, let it go), in order that your Father Who is in heaven may also forgive you your [own] failings and shortcomings and let them drop. Mark 11:25

According to the dictionary, *forgive* also means "to renounce anger or resentment against, to absolve from payment of (e.g., a debt)."[3] I like the phrase used by *The Amplified Bible* in this verse, "Let it drop."

How many times have you had a problem with someone and think you have settled it between you, but the other person keeps bringing it back up?

My husband and I have had those kinds of experiences with each other many times in our shared life.

I believe most men are more willing and able to let things go than women. The popular stereotype of the nagging wife is not entirely inaccurate. I know, because I used to be one of them.

Dave and I would have a disagreement or problem between us and he would say, "Oh, let's just forget about it." But I would keep dragging it up again and again. I can remember him saying to me in desperation, "Joyce, can't we just drop it?"

That's what Jesus is telling us to do here in this verse. Drop it, leave it, let it go, stop talking about it.

But the question is, how do we do that?

RECEIVE THE HOLY SPIRIT

Then Jesus said to them again, Peace to you! [Just] as the Father has sent Me forth, so I am sending you.

And having said this, He breathed on them and said to them, Receive (admit) the Holy Spirit!

[Now having received the Holy Spirit, and being led and directed by Him] if you forgive the sins of anyone, they are forgiven; if you retain the sins of anyone, they are retained. John 20:21-23

The number one rule in forgiving sins is to receive the Holy Spirit Who provides the strength and ability to forgive.

None of us can do that on our own.

I believe when Jesus breathed on the disciples and they received the Holy Spirit, they were born again at that moment. The very next thing He said to them was whatever sins they forgave were forgiven and whatever sins they retained were retained.

The forgiving of sins seems to be the first power conferred upon people when they become born again. If that is so, then the forgiving of sins is our first duty as believers. But though we have the *power* to forgive sins, it is not always *easy* to forgive sins.

Whenever someone does something to me I need to forgive, I pray, "Holy Spirit, breathe on me and give me the strength to forgive this person." I do that because my emotions are screaming and yelling, "You have hurt me — and that's not fair!"

At that point I have to remember what we have already learned about letting go and allowing the God of justice to "even the score" and work out everything in the end. I have to remind myself that my job is to pray, His job is to pay.

When someone does something hurtful to you, go to the Lord and receive from Him the strength to place your will on the altar and say, "Lord, I forgive this person. I loose him; I let him go."

Once you have done that, you have to let it drop. It does no good to go through all that then go to lunch with friends or associates and rehash the whole thing. Why? Because Satan will use it as an opportunity to nullify your decision to forgive and rob you of your peace and blessing.

SATAN WILL BAIT YOU!
ᢞ

Understand [this], my beloved brethren.
Let every man be quick to hear [a ready listener],

slow to speak, slow to take offense and to get angry.
James 1:19

It is very important to understand that Satan will bait you
— even through the mouth of other Christians.

Do you know what they will say to you at lunch?

"So how are you and so-and-so getting along? I heard you two
were having a little problem."

See the tempting bait?

Since you are trying to forget it, you may respond, "Oh, no
harm was intended."

But if you are not careful, the others will continue to bait you
with questions, drawing you into a conversation about a subject
you have determined to drop.

I know how gossip works because in my earlier years I could
not walk away from a juicy story. Someone would say something
to me about somebody else, and my ears would practically stand
out on my head. I would get all excited, "Oh, I'm about to learn a
secret!" That's the kind of thing that poisons us.

Now whenever anyone begins to talk about someone else
or another ministry, I try to turn the conversation in a totally
different direction. I pass it off by saying something like, "Well,
I just pray that God will help that person and ministry to
work through their problems and learn something from this
experience that will make them more powerful than ever."

When someone comes to you to bait you into talking about
some problem in your church or ministry, you need to try to turn
the conversation by saying, "Oh yes, that's right, we did have a
little problem for a while. But as far as I am concerned, everything
is going to work out fine."

If that person insists on asking how things are going, let him know politely but firmly that you are not going to discuss it negatively in any way.

Do as the Bible says and be slow to speak, quick to hear, and slow to take offense or get angry.

Whenever you hear something that upsets you and causes you to want to react rashly, stop and think, "What's the devil trying to do to me here?"

What he is probably trying to do is to nullify your prayer of forgiveness by baiting you into rehearsing the offense over and over again.

What good does it do any of us to tell somebody else how bad we have been hurt? Now I am not saying we should never share with our spouse or minister or close friend what is happening in our life. But we must preserve a balance here. We must be careful not to destroy someone else's character or reputation. Just because someone has wronged us does not give us the right to wrong that person in return. Two wrongs don't make a right.

Forgive to keep Satan from getting the advantage over you. Refuse to take the devil's bait. Don't keep rehearsing the offense. If you really want to get over something hurtful, then stop thinking and talking about it.

A TONE OF MERCY

And when they came to the place which is called
The Skull [Latin: Calvary; Hebrew: Golgotha], there
they crucified Him, and [along with] the criminals,
one on the right and one on the left.

And Jesus prayed, Father, forgive them, for they
know not what they do.... Luke 23:33,34

I have shared this example often, but I am sharing it again because I believe it is a very powerful one.

My husband's mother raised eight children almost single-handedly. Today all of those children are serving the Lord.

While they were little, she had to clean other people's homes just to make ends meet because she was not on any kind of government welfare program. All she had to support herself and her family was a small monthly Social Security check. As the older children grew up, they helped her and the rest of the family. Everyone did what he could to bring in some money.

That environment in which Dave grew up would be called poor by today's standards. But all of those children knew they were loved. They were taken to church and taught Christian values and principles. And that upbringing has had a lasting effect upon each of them.

In all the years Dave and I have been married, I have never heard him or any of his family members say one downgrading thing about their dad, even though he was the one most responsible for their difficult situation all that time. He was in bondage to alcohol and died when Dave was sixteen years old. His family has always presented the issue with a tone of mercy. I believe their forgiving attitude has opened doors of blessing in their lives.

When Jesus was hanging on the cross, He prayed for those who were tormenting Him, saying, "Father, forgive them for they know not what they do." You and I need to clothe ourselves with Jesus, to take on His character and personality. We need to quit being so concerned about what others are doing to *us* and become more concerned with what they are doing to *themselves* by the way they are treating us.

In the Old Testament, the Lord said to the enemies of His

people Israel, ...**Touch not My anointed...** (1 Chron. 16:22). Since you and I are children of God, we are His anointed. People place themselves in a dangerous position when they mistreat us, so we need to pray for them. We need to have mercy on them and do as Jesus did, asking God to forgive them because they do not realize what they are doing.

BLESS, NOT CURSE

Now I would like to cite three very important Scriptures relating to forgiveness to see if you can detect a common thread in each of them that we often overlook in seeking to be able to forgive someone who has hurt us.

> You have heard that it was said, You shall love your neighbor and hate your enemy;
>
> But I tell you, Love your enemies and pray for those who persecute you. Matthew 5:43,44
>
> Invoke blessings upon and pray for the happiness of those who curse you, implore God's blessing (favor) upon those who abuse you [who revile, reproach, disparage, and high-handedly misuse you]. Luke 6:28
>
> Bless those who persecute you [who are cruel in their attitude toward you]; bless and do not curse them. Romans 12:14

Do you see what is missing when we just forgive our enemies and go no further?

Let me share with you a lesson I learned from ministering on this subject of forgiveness.

I once asked the Lord, "Father, why is it that people come to our meetings and pray to be able to learn to forgive, yet in just a short time they are right back again still having problems and asking for help?"

The first thing the Lord told me about such people is this: "They don't do what I tell them in the Word."

You see, although God tells us in His Word to *forgive* others, He does not stop there. He goes on to instruct us to *bless* them.

In this context, the word *bless* means "to speak well of."[4] So one of our problems is that although we pray and forgive those who have offended us, we turn right around and curse them with our tongues or we rehash the offense again and again with others.

That won't work!

To work through the process of forgiveness and enjoy the peace we seek, we must do what God has told us to do, which is not only to forgive but also to bless.

One reason we find it so hard to pray for those who have hurt us and mistreated us is that we have a tendency to think we are asking God to bless them physically or materially.

The truth is that we are not praying for them to make more money or have more possessions, we are praying for them to be blessed spiritually. What we are doing is asking God to bring truth and revelation to them about their attitude and behavior so they will be willing to repent and be set free from their sins.

I know how hard it can be to speak well of people who have done us wrong. Let me give you an example from my own experience.

Some time ago we moved into a nice house in a new subdivision. The only problem was that the builder of that house did not follow through with all the repairs he had promised to make. So we ended up having to spend extra time and money fixing up things that should not have been our responsibility. But we were determined not to "bad mouth" him. Why? Because we didn't want Satan to get the advantage over us.

One evening I saw a young woman out taking her little boy for a walk near our home, so I struck up a conversation with her.

"Are you enjoying your new house?" I asked, trying to be friendly.

"Oh, yes," she answered, "but don't get me started on the builder!"

Now this was a sweet lady, but I recognized right away that the devil was trying to bait me. How my flesh would have liked to respond, "Oh, go right ahead — get started!"

I was so tempted to encourage her to start downgrading the builder. But just then it came to me what to say.

"Well," I replied, "I guess it would be hard to find any builder who would do everything 100 percent right."

That remark turned the entire conversation.

It is not enough that we forgive others, we must be careful not to curse them, not to speak evil of them even if it seems they deserve it. Instead, we must do as Jesus did and bless them, speak well of them. Why? Because in so doing, we bless not only them, but also ourselves.

FORGIVING OTHERS AND FORGIVING SELF

...if we [really] are living and walking in the Light, as He [Himself] is in the Light, we have [true, unbroken] fellowship with one another, and the blood of Jesus Christ His Son cleanses (removes) us from all sin and guilt [keeps us cleansed from sin in all its forms and manifestations]....

> If we [freely] admit that we have sinned and
> confess our sins, He is faithful and just (true to His
> own nature and promises) and will forgive our sins
> [dismiss our lawlessness] and [continuously]
> cleanse us from all unrighteousness [everything not
> in conformity to His will in purpose, thought, and
> action]. 1 John 1:7,9

While we are learning to forgive, we must remember we are to forgive not only others but also ourselves. We must accept and receive the forgiveness we ask God to give us.

If we feel that we have done things to cause problems for others, we need to be forgiven just as much as we need to forgive those who have caused problems for us.

If we walk in unforgiveness toward ourselves, we cut ourselves off from fellowship with God just as surely as when we walk in unforgiveness toward others. We must be just as quick to forgive ourselves of our own sins and failures and weaknesses as we are to forgive those who have wronged us. Otherwise, we will end up in the realm of guilt and condemnation.

God wants us to be free so He can have full fellowship with us. But when we are filled with guilt and condemnation, our fellowship with the Father is ruined.

The Lord has promised: **All whom My Father gives (entrusts) to Me will come to Me; and the one who comes to Me I will most certainly not cast out [I will never, no never, reject one of them who comes to Me]** (John 6:37).

If you have done something wrong, go to the Lord. He has promised to forgive you of your sins, to remove them from you as far as the east is from the west, and to remember them no more.

Do you ever forget something important and cannot remember what it was, no matter how hard you try? That's the way God is about our sins. Once we have acknowledged and confessed them, He forgives us of them and forgets them so that He cannot recall them even if He tries.

According to the Bible, there is no condemnation to those who are in Christ Jesus; old things have passed away, and all things have been made new. (Rom. 8:1; 2 Cor. 5:17.)

So why not do yourself a favor and forgive yourself just as you forgive others?

FORGIVING GOD

Another area in which many people have problems is unforgiveness toward God.

Those who have never experienced that feeling may not understand it. But those who have know what it is to feel animosity toward God because they blame Him for cheating them out of something important in their lives. Things have not worked out the way they had planned. They figure that God could have changed things if He had wanted to, but since He didn't they blame Him for the situation in which they find themselves. They feel God has disappointed them and let them down.

You may have felt that way at one time or another in your life. If so, you know it is impossible to have fellowship with someone you are mad at. In that case, the only answer is to forgive God!

Again, that may sound strange, and, of course, God does not need to be forgiven! But such honesty can break the bondage and restore the fellowship that has been broken by anger toward the Lord.

Often we think we could accept things better if only we knew why they have turned out the way they have. We think if we just knew *why* certain things have happened to us, we would be satisfied. But the Lord shared with me that we might be much less satisfied if we really knew.

I believe God tells us only what we really need to know, what we are prepared to handle, what will not harm us but will, in fact, help us.

Many times we go digging around trying to discover something that God is withholding from us for our own good. That's why we must learn to trust God and not try to figure out everything in life.

Sooner or later, we must come to the place where we stop feeling bitter, resentful, and sorry for ourselves. There must come a time when we stop living in the past and asking why. Instead, we must learn to let God turn our scars into stars.

BINDING AND LOOSING BY FORGIVING

> Verily I say unto you, Whatsoever ye shall bind
> on earth shall be bound in heaven: and whatsoever
> ye shall loose on earth shall be loosed in heaven.
> Matthew 18:18 KJV

We have not heard enough messages on forgiveness. We need to grow to the point of being quick to forgive, and hearing more on the subject will strengthen us to do so.

It is true that you and I have authority as believers, the authority to bind and to loose. We have been taught that truth from Matthew 18:18. However if you read the entire eighteenth chapter of Matthew, you will see that in it Jesus is actually talking about *forgiveness*!

In verse 21 Peter asked Jesus how many times he should forgive his brother who sins against him. In His answer Jesus told the story of the servant who was forgiven by his master of a huge unpayable debt. But then the man went out and demanded immediate payment from another servant who owed him a tiny sum, threatening to have him and his family thrown into jail if he could not pay. The end result was that the evil servant was called in before his master and condemned to debtors' prison because he had refused to forgive someone else just as he had been forgiven. (vv. 23-34.)

Then in the last verse Jesus concluded this entire chapter by saying, **So also My heavenly Father will deal with every one of you if you do not freely forgive your brother from your heart his offenses** (v. 35).

In verses 15 through 17, just before the verse on binding and loosing, Jesus taught if our brother wrongs us, then we are to go to him privately and try to settle the matter. If he won't listen, then we are to take two others with us. If he still won't listen, we are to bring the issue before the church. If he still won't listen, then we are to break fellowship with him.

But do you realize that all of that is for our brother's sake and not for our own?

All of it!

I do believe there is a time when we may have to break fellowship with someone, but it should be for his benefit and not for ours — to help him realize the severity of his wrong behavior and, hopefully, repent and manifest godly behavior. Many times when people have a problem, they won't do anything about it until something like a broken fellowship forces them to assess the situation and take action to set things right.

FORGIVENESS AND RESTORATION

Does forgiveness mean restoration?

Many people have the mistaken idea that if someone has hurt them and they forgive that person, they will have to go back and suffer through the same hurt all over again. They believe that in order to forgive, they must enter back into an active relationship with the person who has injured them.

That is not true, and this misconception has caused a problem for many people who want to forgive.

Forgiveness does not necessarily mean restoration. If the relationship can be restored, and it is within God's will for it to be restored, then restoration is the best plan. But a broken relationship cannot always be restored. Sometimes it would not even be wise, especially in cases where abuse has been involved.

CLEANSING THE WOUND

Someone in my early life abused me for a long period of time. I came to hate him. Finally, years later, God sovereignly delivered me from that hatred because I gave it to Him and asked Him to set me free from it.

Although I had forgiven the person and was free of my hatred of him, I still did not want to be around him.

Even though we make the decision to forgive someone, it may take a long time before our emotions are healed in that area.

God revealed to me that forgiving is like cleaning out the infection in a wound. The Word of God helps us renew our minds concerning how to properly dress an emotional wound. But how deep the scar goes depends a great deal on how well the wound is treated in its initial stages.

If a wound is properly cared for from the beginning, the scar left from it will not cause a problem. If it is left unattended and the infection is allowed to grow and spread, even though the wound is cleaned out and bandaged, a nasty scar may remain that can cause problems later on.

The same is true emotionally as well as physically. The best plan is quick and complete forgiveness; however, many people don't realize that when they initially get hurt. If a person has not been taught godly principles and guidelines, he reacts in a natural human way, as I did when I was abused. All I knew was hatred for my abuser, and the result was a hard heart, rebellion, and many other problems that have taken years to overcome.

It is more difficult to recover if the wound has been deep and left scars. But God promises to bring restoration in our lives, and I know from personal experience that He does what He promises to do if we do what He tells us to do.

We can decide to forgive others and refuse to speak evil of them as God's Word instructs us. We can pray for them and ask God to bless them. We can even do all kinds of good deeds for them and show them mercy and grace. Yet we can still *feel* wounded by them. It takes time for our feelings to catch up with our decisions.

Even after a physical wound appears to be healed on the outside, it can still be sore and tender on the inside. It is the same with emotional wounds. For this reason we must be able to distinguish true forgiveness from feelings that are still sore and tender.

FORGIVENESS VERSUS FEELINGS

I believe the greatest deception in the area of forgiveness Satan has perpetuated in the Church is the idea that if a person's *feelings* have not changed, he has not forgiven.

Many people believe this deception. They decide to forgive someone who has harmed them, but the devil convinces them that because they still have the same feelings toward the person, they have not fully forgiven that individual.

They go back to square one and begin praying the same prayer all over again: "Oh, God, what's wrong with me? I want to forgive, but I just can't! Help me, Lord. Please help me!"

In my own case, although I forgave the person who had abused me and eventually tried to have fellowship with him, he made it clear he did not think he had ever done anything wrong. In fact, he even went so far as to blame me for what happened. I was finally forced to do as Jesus taught in Matthew 18 and cut off fellowship with him until he came to repentance.

It would have been unwise to try to reconcile the relationship if there was no repentance on his part. Until people repent, they usually do the same things again and again. I knew that I had to protect myself and that it was not God's will for me to open the door for more abuse.

At one point I told him, "I want you to know that I am through being abused by you. You have controlled me for a long time, but no longer. I love you as someone for whom Jesus died, and I am willing to go forward with our relationship, but until you acknowledge your sins against me and repent of them, it is impossible for us to have a proper relationship."

Confronting him in this manner was something I was led

to do by the Spirit of God, and it was part of my own healing process.

I had been controlled by a spirit of fear where this person was concerned for many years, and it was time to confront that fear.

Does all this mean that I was filled with bitterness, resentment, and unforgiveness? No, it just means that I was able to distinguish between my forgiveness and my feelings. I forgave him because I love God and want to do what He tells me to do. It took a long time for my feelings to catch up with my decision because of the depth of the wound, but I had done my part. I had acted on the Word of God and made the decision to forgive. Restoration was not possible yet, but forgiveness was.

If we do what we can do, God will always do what we cannot do. I could make a decision to obey God, but I could not change how I felt. God did that for me as time went by.

Healing takes time!

We can cleanse and disinfect the wound. We can bandage it and tend it. But we cannot actually heal it. Jesus is the Healer.

There is a good conclusion to my story! Later God moved in a mighty way to bring deliverance and healing to this relationship. The Lord had been working behind the scenes, and one day the person who had abused me told me he was sorry that what he had done had hurt me. He said that he never intended to hurt me and that although he had known that what he was doing was wrong, he had never really understood how badly it would affect me.

At the time I had already forgiven him from my heart, but this admission of wrongdoing on his part and his willingness to try to do right opened the door for the beginning of restoration in the relationship. It has been slow and not always comfortable, but at least we have been progressively moving forward.

I have included this example from my own life to help you realize that just because you will to forgive does not mean that you no longer have any feelings. You may hurt for a long time. But the important thing is not to allow the enemy to convince you that just because your feelings are wounded, you have not done your part before God.

Remember, decide to forgive, pray for your enemies, bless and do not curse them. Be good to those who have mistreated you because you overcome evil with good (see Rom. 12:21). And wait for God to take care of your feelings.

With the help of God we can learn to manage our emotions even though they may be tender and hurting. With the power of the Holy Spirit helping us, we can learn not to mistreat those who have hurt us. We can avoid saying unkind things about them to others. We can pray for them. We can wait for God's recompense and see His glory manifested in our lives by choosing to do things His way!

5
MOOD SWINGS
ॐ

The ups and downs in our emotions is one of the major tools Satan uses to steal our joy and destroy our effectiveness as witnesses for Christ. We need to learn to become stable, solid, steadfast, persevering, determined believers.

As we noted in the very beginning of this book, none of us is ever going to be totally rid of emotions. But thank God we can learn to manage those emotions. We can learn to control our emotions and not let them control us.

Life is no fun when it is controlled by feelings, because feelings change from day to day, hour to hour, even moment to moment. Feelings cannot be trusted, not only because they change so often, but because they also lie.

The devil loves to use our feelings to influence us because he knows we are "soulish" creatures. Too often we allow ourselves to be guided by our soul — our mind, will, and emotions — rather than by the Spirit of Truth.

We cannot stop the enemy from placing negative thoughts in our mind, but we don't have to dwell on those thoughts. Because we have a will, we can choose to refuse them. In the same way, we cannot stop Satan from playing on our emotions, but we can use that same will to refuse to give in to our emotions.

The fact is that, as followers of Christ, we must live by truth and wisdom, not by feelings and emotions.

REASONING WITH SELF

In order to live by truth and wisdom, sometimes we have to reason with ourselves.

When strange feelings threaten to overwhelm us, we need to stop and take control of our thoughts and feelings. One way we do that is by talking to ourselves either silently or out loud.

I do that all the time.

There was a time in my life when I did not resist negative feelings and, as a result, I had a very unstable, miserable life.

Now when feelings of loneliness begin to rise up within me to cause me fear and misery, I stop and say to myself: "Joyce Meyer, knock it off! You may *feel* lonely, but you are *not* lonely. With all the people God has placed in your life to love and care for you, you can't possibly be lonely."

So even though I may occasionally feel lonely, I don't allow my feelings to dictate to me and spoil my life. That is part of what is called emotional maturity.

EMOTIONAL MATURITY

You may be in a crowd of people and *feel* everybody is talking about you, but that doesn't mean they are.

You may *feel* nobody understands you, but that doesn't mean they don't.

You may *feel* you are misunderstood, unappreciated, or even mistreated, but that doesn't mean it is true.

Satan wants us to listen to our feelings which are changeable and unreliable rather than listening to the voice of the Holy Spirit Who always speaks the truth. For that reason we need to make emotional maturity our goal. And for the believer, the first step to emotional maturity is learning to listen to the Spirit rather than the soul.

If we want to be mature, disciplined, Spirit-controlled people, we must be *determined* to walk in the Spirit and not in the flesh. It takes a constant act of the will to choose to do things God's way rather than our way.

LIKE A ROCK

And they all drank the same spiritual (supernaturally given) drink. For they drank from a spiritual Rock which followed them [produced by the sole power of God Himself without natural instrumentality], and *the Rock was Christ.* 1 Corinthians 10:4

My husband has always been very stable emotionally. In fact, he reminds me of a rock, which is one of the names of Jesus.

One way of explaining the nature of Jesus would be to say that He has emotional maturity. Part of that maturity is stability, being unchanging.

The writer of the book of Hebrews tells us that **Jesus Christ (the Messiah) is [always] the same, yesterday, today, [yes] and forever (to the ages)** (Heb. 13:8).

Do you really believe that Jesus allowed Himself to be moved or led around by His emotions, as we so often do? Of course not. We know that He was led by the Spirit, not by feelings, though we have seen that He was subject to all the same feelings you and I experience in our daily lives.

In that sense, Dave has always been much more like Jesus than I have. Dave is as stable and unchanging as a rock. It is comfortable to live with somebody like that because you always know what to expect.

To tell the truth, I used to get aggravated with Dave at times because he never got excited or upset about anything. It was just part of his phlegmatic personality not to show much emotion. On the other hand, I more than made up for it by constantly going from one extreme to the other, up and down like a roller coaster.

Do you know when my emotional roller coaster finally began to level off? It started when I began to put my foot down and make a determined decision that with the help of the Holy Spirit I was not going to be that way anymore.

Until I decided I was through living by my feelings, I was in bondage to my emotions. I would be up one day, laughing and feeling good, then down the next, weeping and crying and feeling sorry for myself. The following day I would bounce back for a while, only to turn around and fall right back into misery. I reached the point of not wanting to have to face any type of change in my life because I knew it would bring on all kinds of emotional problems I was not prepared to handle. I then realized that what I needed was emotional maturity and stability.

Dave provided an excellent example of what that was, and observing him made me desire the same emotional maturity and stability I saw him display.

We all need to be stable.

Too often we make prosperity or success or something else our goal when our first objective should be emotional maturity. Although we cannot achieve that maturity and stability on our own, God will help us if we truly desire change.

YOUR GOD IS MIGHTY

The Lord thy God in the midst of thee is mighty.... Zephaniah 3:17 KJV

In the Old Testament, Elisha attached himself to the prophet Elijah and became his follower and disciple because he wanted to be strong in the Lord like his master.

If you have an emotional problem, then you need to stop associating with people who are worse off than you are. Instead, you need to spend time with those who are spiritually and emotionally mature.

I knew that I might never be as emotionally strong and stable as Dave because we are of two totally different personality types. But I was determined I was going to come to the place of not being tormented and controlled by my emotions.

The Scriptures tell us that the Lord our God Who resides within each of us is "mighty." Mighty to do what? One way He is "mighty" in us is to help us overcome our emotions and be led by His unchangeable Word and Spirit and not by our unstable feelings and emotions.

Your God is able. Why not trust Him to help you develop the same kind of emotional maturity and stability that marked the life of His own Son, Jesus Christ, our hope of glory?

CHRIST: THE HOPE OF GLORY

...God was pleased to make known how great
for the Gentiles are the riches of the glory of this
mystery, which is *Christ* within and among you, *the
Hope of* [realizing the] *glory.* Colossians 1:27

As believers, our only hope of glory is Christ Jesus. Only He
can provide us what we need to live joyfully and victoriously in
this life.

As we have seen, Jesus is called the Rock because He was solid
and stable — always the same, never changing. He was not moved
by all the things that move us. People could try to push Him off a
cliff, and He would walk right through their midst.

How was He able to do things like that? He was able to do
that because He knew He was in God's hands and that nobody
could do anything to Him out of God's will and timing. He rested
in that knowledge, and it gave Him an unshakable sense of peace
and security. In Mark 4 He was able to speak peace to the storm
because He never allowed the storm to get inside Him. He re-
mained calm!

That is more or less the same kind of attitude and outlook I
have seen in my husband Dave. If we had money problems, I
would get all worried, not knowing what was going to become of
us. But Dave would simply say, "Joyce, we're tithing and doing
everything the Lord has told us to do. God has always met our
needs before, and He will meet them this time too. Why should
we sit around and be miserable, trying to figure out what to do?
Let's just relax and trust the Lord to handle everything."

If someone began to talk negatively about us or came against
us or tried to stir up strife against us, I would get all nervous and
upset. But Dave would be totally unruffled.

I would say, "Dave, doesn't all this drive you nuts!"

"No," he would answer. "We don't have a problem, it's all these people who have the problem. Our heart is right before the Lord, so why should we get all bothered?"

With most of us, that kind of spiritual stability and emotional maturity doesn't come naturally. We have to desire it with all our heart. We have to determine that whatever it takes, we are going to have it. We have to develop a hunger for it, like the hunger for righteousness that Jesus spoke of in the Sermon on the Mount. (Matt. 5:6).

We have to get to the point that we are determined to *enjoy* our spiritual inheritance.

EMOTIONAL STABILITY AS A SPIRITUAL INHERITANCE

> In Him we also were made [God's] heritage (portion) and we obtained an inheritance; for we had been foreordained (chosen and appointed beforehand) in accordance with His purpose, Who works out everything in agreement with the counsel and design of His [own] will,
>
> So that we who first hoped in Christ [who first put our confidence in Him have been destined and appointed to] live for the praise of His glory!
> Ephesians 1:11,12

We have got to get to the point of knowing who we are in Christ and what is rightfully ours because we have placed our confidence in Him.

Emotional stability is part of our spiritual inheritance.

We do not have to live on an emotional roller coaster in which our feelings go up and down from one day to the next. Instead, we are to live as Christ lived, with a sense of peace and security that comes from knowing who we are and Whose we are.

Until we make the decision to claim and live in our inheritance, the enemy will continue to rob us of what Jesus died to provide for us — His peace and joy that prevail within us even in the midst of the turmoil and confusion and fear that surround us on all sides.

In John 16:33 Jesus said, "In the world you will have tribulation. Cheer up! I have overcome the world." We cannot cheer up until we calm down. We can enjoy life even if all our circumstances aren't great. Yet we cannot have joy without peace.

THE GOAL OF EMOTIONAL STABILITY

My son David and I have the same type of strong choleric personality, so we often got into screaming matches with each other before we learned to submit our personalities to the Lord.

Before I learned to depend on the Holy Spirit to help me control my emotional outbursts, I was under constant condemnation. I finally stopped feeling guilty for my emotional lapses when I realized I was a human being with a weak nature and if I had been perfect I would not have had a need for a Perfect Savior.

Jesus came to be the Perfect Sacrifice for us because we do not have the ability to be perfect in our natural man. We need to remember that fact when we are tempted to be overcome by guilt and condemnation every time we fail to control our emotions.

Through a series of painful experiences with my son, I learned that a little humility teaches a far greater lesson that warfare. David began to change when I began to change, and I began to change when I finally came to realize that although I have emotions, I don't have to give in to them.

The point I am making is not that I never have negative emotions anymore, but that it has become my goal to control my emotions, not the other way around. But until I got to the place that I wanted to stop giving in to my emotions of anger, self-pity, and depression, I was a mess.

What I had to do was set for myself the *goal* of emotional stability. I had to learn to seek not to be emotionless, but rather to be well-balanced in my emotional life.

WELL-BALANCED

Be *well balanced* (temperate, sober of mind), be vigilant and cautious at all times; for that enemy of yours, the devil, roams around like a lion roaring [in fierce hunger], seeking someone to seize upon and devour.

Withstand him; be firm in faith [against his onset — rooted, established, strong, immovable, and determined], knowing that the same (identical) sufferings are appointed to your brotherhood (the whole body of Christians) throughout the world. 1 Peter 5:8,9

To be temperate is to be self-controlled. And to be sober of mind is to be level-headed.

So here you and I are told to be well-balanced, self-controlled, level-headed, rooted, established, strong, immovable, and determined.

According to this passage, how are we going to defeat the devil and withstand his physical and emotional onsets upon us? By being rooted and grounded in Christ. Satan may come against us with feelings, but we don't have to submit to our emotions. We can stand firmly against them even while they rage against us and even within us.

CONSTANCY AND FEARLESSNESS

...do not [for a moment] be frightened or intimidated in anything by your opponents and adversaries, for such [*constancy* and *fearlessness*] will be a clear sign (proof and seal) to them of [their impending] destruction, but [a sure token and evidence] of your deliverance and salvation, and that from God. Philippians 1:28

Notice those two words "constancy" and "fearlessness." They describe the rock-like temperament you and I are to display in the face of attacks and onslaughts by our opponents and adversaries — both physical and spiritual.

When people or events come against us to destroy us, we are to stand firm, confident everything is going to work out for the best. We are not to change, but rather to remain constant and let God do the changing — of the circumstances.

When problems arise — and they will from time to time — we are not to assume that the Lord will intervene without an invitation and take care of all our problems for us. We are to pray and ask Him to change our circumstances. Then we are to remain constant and unchanging, which will be a sign to the enemy of his impending downfall and destruction.

Do you know why our constancy and fearlessness are a sign to Satan that he will fail? Because he knows that the only way he can overcome a believer is through deception and intimidation. How can he threaten someone who has no fear of him? How can he deceive someone who recognizes his lies and refuses to believe them? What good does it do him to try to stir up fear or anger or depression in someone who will not be moved by emotions but who chooses to stand firmly on the Word of God?

When the devil sees his tactics are not working, he realizes he is failing and will be utterly defeated.

A good example of this type of fearless constancy in the face of frightening circumstances is found in the book of Exodus when the Children of Israel stood on the banks of the Red Sea and saw the army of Pharaoh coming after them to destroy them.

> Moses told the people, Fear not; stand still (firm, confident, undismayed) and see the salvation of the Lord which He will work for you today. For the Egyptians you have seen today you shall never see again.
>
> The Lord will fight for you, and you shall hold your peace and remain at rest. Exodus 14:13,14

When confronted with a situation like the one that the Israelites faced in this passage, we are to do what they were told to do: remain constant, hold our peace, stand at rest, and let God do our fighting for us.

KEEPING CALM IN THE DAY OF ADVERSITY

> Blessed (happy, fortunate, to be envied) is the man whom You discipline and instruct, O Lord, and teach out of Your law,

That You may give him power to keep himself *calm in the days of adversity*, until the [inevitable] pit of corruption is dug for the wicked.

For the Lord will not cast off nor spurn His people, neither will He abandon His heritage.

For justice will return to the [uncompromisingly] righteous, and all the upright in heart will follow it. Psalm 94:12-15

What is the Lord saying to us here in this passage? He is saying that He deals with us and disciplines us for a reason. He does that so we will come to the point where we can keep ourselves calm in the day of adversity.

In verses 14 and 15 notice the emphasis on God's faithfulness and justice toward us, His inheritance, the uncompromisingly righteous. We can be sure that if we are being obedient to the Word and will of God and are being led by His Holy Spirit, we have nothing to fear from our enemies, because the Lord Himself will fight our battles for us.

But we must want to be helped. As we have seen, even God cannot help someone who doesn't really want to be helped. If you and I really want to be helped, then we must remain stable as we wait upon Him to move in our behalf

REMAINING STABLE

He who dwells in the secret place of the Most High shall remain stable and fixed under the shadow of the Almighty [Whose power no foe can withstand]. Psalm 91:1

When you and I feel a tide of emotions beginning to rise up within us, we need to return to the secret place of the Most High, crying out to Him: "Father, help me to resist this surge of emotions that threatens to overwhelm me!"

If we will do that, the Lord has promised to intervene on our behalf. We need to learn to take refuge under His shadow, where we will be safe and secure, knowing that no power in heaven or on earth can withstand Him.

Avoiding Emotional Highs and Lows

In our efforts to develop emotional maturity, we must be careful to avoid both extremes: highs and lows.

Most of us have heard a great deal of teaching about emotional lows such as discouragement, depression, despondency, and despair. But the Lord has revealed to me that we also need to avoid the other extreme, which is emotional highs.

God has shown me that if we give in to extreme highs we are as out of balance as we are when we give in to extreme lows. To maintain an emotional balance, we need to stay on a level plain, somewhere between both extremes.

It may be hard for some people to maintain emotional stability because they are addicted to excitement. For some reason, they just can't seem to settle down and live ordinary, everyday lives like everyone else.

Such people have to have something exciting going on all the time. If they don't, they soon get bored and start looking for something to "turn them on." Their search for excitement often leads to excessive emotional stimulation, not to the steady, deep-seated joy that is supposed to characterize the life of the believer.

It is not wrong to be excited, but it is dangerous to be excessive.

JOY AS CALM DELIGHT

I have told you these things, that My joy and delight may be in you, and that your joy and gladness may be full measure and complete and overflowing. John 15:11

Sometimes we believers seem to think that in order to be filled with the joy of the Lord we have to be turned-on, fired-up, and super-hyped!

Jesus did tell us that His joy and delight are to be in us to the full measure. But that does not mean that we are to swing from chandeliers!

I know that the word *joy* has often been defined by some teachers and ministers as "hilarity," and there is some basis for that definition. But according to Strong's concordance, the actual meaning of the Greek word *chara* translated *joy* in John 15:11 is "calm delight."[1]

I like that definition because I have seen it displayed in my own marriage. For more than thirty years I have watched my husband Dave live a life of calm delight, and it has been a great blessing to me.

Dave likens this kind of calm delight to a bubbling brook that just flows along quietly and peacefully, bringing refreshment to everything and everyone along its path.

Yet so many of us are like the ocean. Our emotions come in and go out like the roaring tide. One moment we are surging forward overflowing everything in our path, and the next moment we are rushing back out leaving debris everywhere.

After years of living that kind of ebb-and-flow life, I came to want so much to be able to have the kind of peaceful existence that marked the life of my husband. I understand the stress and turmoil that can be caused by excessive highs and lows.

I am not saying that it is wrong to ever get excited. But I am saying that we need to be careful about becoming all "hyped up," because invariably hype leads to disillusionment and disappointment.

BE ADAPTABLE AND ADJUSTABLE

Rejoice with those who rejoice [sharing others' joy], and weep with those who weep [sharing others' grief].

Live in harmony with one another; do not be haughty (snobbish, high-minded, exclusive), but readily adjust yourself to [people, things] and give yourselves to humble tasks. Never over-estimate yourself or be wise in your own conceits.
Romans 12:15,16

There is a balance that needs to be maintained in this very delicate area of appropriate emotional responses.

For example, when Dave surprised me with the beautiful 14-karat gold watch I had wanted so badly, I was filled with joy, meaning that I had calm delight about it. I thanked God that I had a husband who loved me enough to do such nice things for me. I also thanked the Lord that I had had the sense to let Him work out His plan for me, instead of trying to do it myself. If I had bought the one I thought I was able to afford, I would have ended up with a cheap watch that I would not have been happy with very long.

Although I was delighted, I did not do what I would have done ten years earlier. I did not run to the office and show everyone what I had on my wrist. In fact, I disciplined myself not to tell anybody about it but my children and closest friends.

If someone noticed and said, "Oh, you've got a new watch," I would say, "Yes, Dave bought it for me. Wasn't that sweet of him?"

Many times we take away the joy and blessedness that should exist between us and the Lord because when He does something special for us we run all over town enthusiastically boasting to people about what has happened.

But that is not the end of the story. The very next morning I noticed that the watch wasn't keeping proper time.

I thought, "Oh, Dave didn't set it right."

I pulled out the stem to set the watch, and the stem wouldn't turn the hands. I wouldn't say that I was discouraged, but it was a bit of a disappointment.

My daughter Sandy said to me, "Mom, you sure are being calm for somebody who just got an expensive watch and found out it's not working."

Do you know why I was acting that way? Because since I had not let myself get overly excited about the watch in the first place, I wasn't overly distressed when it didn't work right. Had I run around showing it off and bragging about it to everyone, I would have allowed it to become the center of my joy. Then when I discovered that it wasn't working, I would have been crushed, and my joy would have gone down the drain.

We need to learn to enjoy life and the nice things that come to us in it without getting all emotional.

Let me give you another example.

Some time ago we bought a new house just as I was learning what I am sharing with you about calm delight. People kept asking me, "Are you excited about your new house?" The truth is that I wasn't excited. I had a calm delight, but I was not the least bit excited.

I knew the house was a gift from the Lord, and I thankfully accepted it as such. I had a peace about it, but that was all.

We had lived in the previous house for seventeen years, so it was time for a change. The new house was also a good financial investment for us. So for those reasons I was filled with calm delight, but I really was not emotionally excited at all. Neither did I grieve and mourn when I left our home of seventeen years. Our children were babies there. The first Bible study I taught was there, plus other memories. But I was determined not to be worn out emotionally by the time we moved into our new house.

I had learned to adapt and adjust to my changing circumstances without getting all emotional.

EMOTIONAL BOREDOM

When you first start giving up emotional hype, for a while you may feel *bored*.

For several months after the Lord brought me out of emotional hype and into calm delight I literally had to fight off the thought, "This is boring."

The reason is that, like many other Christians, I had become addicted to emotion.

EMOTIONAL ADDICTIONS

I had spent so many years worrying and fretting, figuring and reasoning, conniving and manipulating, riding the crests and troughs of emotional waves, that when my mind was brought down to a calm delight, my flesh went into trauma.

The Lord used that experience to teach me an important lesson. He showed me many of us have emotional addictions.

Like many others, I was so addicted to worry that if I didn't have anything to worry about I would worry about not having any worries! Other people are so addicted to guilt that if they haven't done anything to be guilty of, they feel guilty about not feeling guilty!

In the same way it is possible to get addicted to excitement. Just as a drug addict runs around looking for a chemical "fix," excitement addicts run around looking for an excitement "fix." Some people just don't know how to live ordinary, everyday lives.

Others are so compulsively goal-oriented that they are always looking for some new challenge. As soon as they have attained one objective, they are bored again until they can find some new goal to reach for.

One young man like that who went to work for us told me one day, "I think I'm finally beginning to grasp something that has been really hard for me to get through my head."

"What's that?" I asked.

"I guess I'm finally beginning to learn that a lot of life is just getting up and going to bed, getting up and going to bed."

If we goal-oriented types could ever learn that truth, we could save ourselves and everyone around us a lot of headaches!

We may not all be called to some great earth-shaking work. The anointing of God does come for great works, but it also comes to help us supernaturally enjoy ordinary, everyday life.

As Christians, we are called to love God, to fellowship with Him and our fellowman, to be a blessing everywhere we go, to bring a little joy into people's lives, to live in harmony with our spouse, to raise the kids that He gives us, and to just keep "getting up and going to bed" — and to do it joyfully unto Him. Psalm 100:2 tells us to serve the Lord with gladness!

There will be days when God brings excitement into our lives, but we should not spend our entire lifetime seeking after such emotional highs.

Sometimes my meetings are exciting, and I appreciate it when that happens. I figure the Lord knew I needed that bit of encouragement to keep me going.

But even there we have to be careful, because excitement creates a hunger for more and more excitement. If we are not careful, we will end up seeking excitement rather than seeking the will of God. We can begin to think that if a church service was not exciting something was wrong. I may leave a meeting I have attended feeling very satisfied yet not excited.

You and I need to learn not to be so affected by our outward circumstances.

Not every one of my meetings is gloriously exciting. New houses come along only once or twice in a lifetime. It is only rarely that we are surprised with a new gold watch. Many days come and go without any great emotional fanfare. But remember, we are anointed with the Holy Spirit to properly handle ordinary, everyday life.

The place where we get into trouble is when there is nothing going on — so we try to start something. We do need some variety in our daily routine. But we also need to learn to be led by the Spirit and not by our own emotional addictions.

Not every day is a holiday. Not every meal is a banquet. Not every event is an extravaganza. Most of the time life just goes along on a regular, even keel.

That's what we should do too. We should learn to take control of our emotions and avoid the mood swings that will keep us from enjoying the continual calm delight that God has planned for us in this life.

6
UNDERSTANDING AND OVERCOMING DEPRESSION

I almost titled this chapter "Uppers and Downers." In fact, I had written that title in my notes, but I changed my mind. I thought you might think this chapter is about drugs, but it is not about drugs at all.

There are a lot of "uppers" and "downers" in this life besides those induced by drugs. In this chapter I intend to show Satan is the one who brings the "downers," and Jesus is the One Who brings the "uppers."

DOWN IN THE PIT

> I waited patiently and expectantly for the Lord;
> and He inclined to me and heard my cry.
>
> He drew me up out of *a horrible pit* [a pit of tumult and of destruction], out of the miry clay (froth and slime), and set my feet upon a rock, steadying my steps and establishing my goings.
> Psalm 40:1,2

When the Bible speaks of "the pit," as in this passage from the book of Psalms, I always think of the depths of depression.

As we will see later, David often spoke of feeling as though he was going down into a pit and calling out to the Lord to rescue him and set his feet on solid, level ground.

Like David, nobody wants to be in the pit of depression. It is a terrible place. I cannot think of a worse place to be. Besides the depression itself, there are the horrible thoughts that Satan calls back to the memory while in that low state.

When we are deeply depressed, we feel bad enough as it is. Then the devil comes along to add to our misery by reminding us of all the horrible things we have ever thought or said or done. His goal is to keep us so miserable and hopeless that we will never rise up to cause him any problems or to fulfill the call of God on our lives.

We must learn to resist descending into the pit of depression where we are at the mercy of the tormentor of our souls who is out to totally destroy us and our witness for Christ.

LEVEL GROUND
∽

Deliver me, O Lord, from my enemies; I flee to
You to hide me.
Teach me to do Your will, for You are my God;
let Your good Spirit lead me into *a level country* and
into the land of uprightness. Psalm 143:9,10

As we saw in the last chapter, if we are to avoid extreme lows, one thing we must do is to avoid extreme highs. We must learn to come into balance. When we get too emotionally high, inevitably we must come down. When we do, often we do not stop at the normal level of emotions — what David called "the level country" — but we continue to plummet into the depths of depression.

I really believe that what David was talking about in Psalm 143 was not actual level ground, but level emotions.

A lady who works with manic-depressives once told me that, in dealing with these types, mental health officials have to not only keep them from sinking into deep depression but also from rising to emotional heights — because one leads to the other. Their goal is to keep patients as much as possible on an even level, a place of steady emotional balance.

As we have seen, as believers, you and I are to keep as much as possible on an even level. We are to avoid getting so addicted to emotionalism that we have to stay constantly on an emotional high or else we risk falling into the depths of depression. Instead of riding on an emotional roller coaster from one extreme to the other, we are to walk in the joy of the Lord, which we have defined as calm delight.

"DOWNERS"

> Why art thou *cast down*, O my soul? and why
> art thou disquieted within me? hope in God: for I
> shall yet praise him, who is the health of my
> countenance, and my God. Psalm 43:5 KJV

According to the concordance, the word "depression" does not appear in the *King James Version* of the Bible. The closest term to appear there is "cast down," as we see in Psalm 43:5 in which David asks, "Why are you cast down, O my soul?"

However, although depression itself is not mentioned by name in the Bible, there are other emotion-related items discussed there such as: despair, discourage(ment), disappoint(ment), destruction, debt, disease, distress, and division. These are just some of the things that Satan uses to try to bring us down into depression.

All these "D words" are what might be called forerunners to depression. Since we all have to be on our guard against them, I have studied each of them to learn more about them and their effect on us as believers.

DESPAIR

> We are hedged in (pressed) on every side [troubled and oppressed in every way], but not cramped or crushed; we suffer embarrassments and are perplexed and unable to find a way out, but not *driven to despair.* 2 Corinthians 4:8

What is despair? According to the dictionary, the verb *despair* means, "To be overcome by a sense of futility or defeat." The noun means, "1. Utter lack of hope. 2. Something destroying all hope."[1] I define it as not knowing what to do, or being utterly without a way.

We all know how frustrated we feel when we know we ought to do something about our situation but don't know what it is. No matter which direction we look, there seems to be no way out.

But for the believer there is always a way out of every situation because Jesus has told us, **I am the Way** (John 14:6).

It gives me great comfort to remember that although there are times when I am like the Apostle Paul — pressed on every side and perplexed because there seems to be no way out of my circumstances — the Lord has promised never to leave me nor forsake me. (Heb. 13:5.) So when I come to a dead end, I am not driven to despair because I know He will show me the way I am to go and will lead me through to victory.

DISAPPOINTMENT, DISCOURAGEMENT, DESTRUCTION

Without counsel purposes are *disappointed*: but in the multitude of counsellors they are established. Proverbs 15:22 KJV

Behold, the Lord thy God hath set the land before thee: go up and possess it, as the Lord God of thy fathers hath said unto thee; fear not, neither be *discouraged*. Deuteronomy 1:21 KJV

Bless the Lord, O my soul....Who redeemeth thy life from *destruction*; who crowneth thee with lovingkindess and tender mercies. Psalm 103:1,4 KJV

All of us become disappointed when we have a plan that fails, a hope that does not materialize, a goal that is unreached.

We are all disappointed when things don't work out the way we wanted them to. We are disappointed by everything from a picnic that is rained out to the sickness or death of a loved one. We are disappointed when the new watch we were given won't run right or when the child we had hoped would turn out right shows no signs of doing so.

When things like that happen, for a certain period of time we experience a let down, one that can lead to depression if it is not handled properly.

That's when we have to make the decision to adapt and adjust, to take a new approach, to just keep going despite our feelings. That's when we must remember that we have the Greater One residing within us, so that no matter what may happen to frustrate us, or how long it may take for our dreams and goals to become reality, we are not going to give up and quit just because of our emotions.

That is when we must remember what God once told me in just such a moment: "When you get disappointed, you can always make the decision to get reappointed!"

Disappointment often leads to discouragement, which is even more of a "downer." We have all experienced the depressing feeling that comes after we have tried our very best to do something and either nothing happens or it all falls totally apart — which is just one form of destruction.

How disappointing and discouraging it is to see the things we love senselessly destroyed by others or, even worse, by our own neglect or failure. Regardless of how it may happen or who may be responsible, it is hard to go on when everything we have counted on falls down around us. That's when those of us who have the creative power of the Holy Spirit on the inside can get a new vision, a new direction, and a new goal to help us overcome the downward pull of disappointment, discouragement, and destruction.

DEBT
ॐ

...pay your debt.... 2 Kings 4:7

We have seen that the Bible teaches us that we are to owe no man anything except to love him. Here in this verse, we see that we are to pay our debts. When we allow debt to overwhelm us, it can bring discouragement and even depression.

Have you realized yet that it is usually emotions out of control that get us into debt? Trying to live beyond our means because we want things for our own personal pleasure or sense of prestige or to impress other people leads to indebtedness.

When Dave and I were young marrieds we got into trouble with debt. We did it by running up our credit cards to the maximum buying things we wanted for ourselves and our children. We were making the minimum payment on the balance each month, but the interest was so high we never seemed to make any progress toward paying off what we owed. In fact, we just kept getting deeper and deeper into debt.

What caused that? Emotions and a lack of wisdom.

If you and I are ever going to get anywhere in the Kingdom of God, we must learn to live by wisdom and not by our carnal desire, which is human emotion. (Prov. 3:13.)

The Bible teaches that Jesus has been made unto us wisdom, and that the Holy Spirit is wisdom within us. (1 Cor. 1:30; Eph. 1:17.) If we will listen to the prompting of the Spirit, we will not get into trouble. But if we live by the dictates of the flesh, we are headed for destruction.

Wisdom makes the decision today it will be comfortable with tomorrow. Emotion does what feels good today and takes no thought of tomorrow. When tomorrow arrives, the wise enjoy it in peace and security, but the foolish end up in discouragement and depression. Why? Because the wise have prepared for tomorrow and are able to enjoy the fruits of their labor, while the foolish who have put pleasure first must now pay for yesterday.

It is much better to work now and play later, than to play now and worry later!

It is so discouraging to go to the mailbox every day and find nothing there but bills, bills, and more bills. Eventually that discouragement leads to depression because of the pressure of not being able to see a way out. When we charge things we cannot pay for, we are spending tomorrow's prosperity today. Then when tomorrow comes, all we have is debt.

How many people are deep in depression right this moment because of overwhelming debt?

To live a disciplined life, which is what it takes to produce good fruit in our lives, we have to be willing to invest today so that we can reap tomorrow.

To relieve the discouragement and depression that come from being in debt, we must get out of debt by becoming self-disciplined to think not of today's sacrifices but of tomorrow's rewards.

DISEASE, DISTRESS, AND DIVISION

By the great force [of my *disease*] my garment is disguised and disfigured; it binds me about like the collar of my coat. Job 30:18

In my *distress* [when seemingly closed in] I called upon the Lord and cried to my God; He heard my voice out of His temple (heavenly dwelling place), and my cry came before Him, into His [very] ears. Psalm 18:6

But I urge and entreat you, brethren, by the name of our Lord Jesus Christ, that all of you be in perfect harmony and full agreement in what you say, and that there be no dissensions or factions or *divisions* among you, but that you be perfectly united in your common understanding and in your opinions and judgments. 1 Corinthians 1:10

The word "disease" simply means dis-ease. It is a minute form of death. If a person feels bad all the time, his dis-ease can easily draw him down into depression. For that reason we say that disease is a "downer."

To be distressed is to feel hindered or to be filled with "anxiety or suffering."[2] That too is a "downer" which can lead to a state of depression if not handled promptly and properly.

As we see in 1 Corinthians 1:10, division refers to dissension, factions, disharmony, disagreement, or strife. To many people like me, division is also a "downer."

I hate disharmony and dissension. I despise arguments and disputes. I can't stand factions and divisions.

I used to be a fighter and was always stirring up something. Now I love peace, harmony, and tranquility. Nothing brings me down worse than division — either within myself or between those I love most, such as my family members. I am sure that God feels the same way about His family.

Division, like all these other "downers," comes from following feelings rather than the Spirit, as we read in James 4:1: **What leads to strife (discord and feuds) and how do conflicts (quarrels and fightings) originate among you? Do they not arise from your sensual desires that are ever warring in your bodily members?**

The end result of all of these "downers" is the same: unsettled emotions, which sooner or later lead to misery and destruction.

"LIFTERS"
꒱

Lord, how are they increased who trouble me!
Many are they who rise up against me.

Many are saying of me, There is no help for
him....

> But You, O Lord, are a shield for me, my glory,
> and *the lifter of my head.* Psalm 3:1-3

Although there are "downers" in this life, there are also "lifters."

In this passage, the psalmist says that despite his distressing situation he is not despairing or becoming depressed because his confidence is the Lord, the lifter of his head.

In Hebrews 12:12 KJV we are told: **Wherefore lift up the hands which hang down....** And in 1 Timothy 2:8 the Apostle Paul wrote: **I desire therefore that in every place men should pray, without anger or quarreling or resentment or doubt [in their minds], lifting up holy hands.**

When we are depressed, everything around us begins to fall apart and lose its strength. Our head and hands and heart all begin to hang down. Even our eyes and our voice are lowered.

This downcast position and stance can depress us even more. When we are in that downcast stance, the Lord tells us, as He did Abraham, **...Lift up now your eyes and look from the place where you are, northward and southward and eastward and westward** (Gen. 13:14).

Our eyes and hearts are downcast because we are looking at the problem rather than at the Lord.

In Genesis 13, we read that the herdsmen of Abraham and his nephew Lot were arguing and fighting because there was not enough room for both of their flocks and herds to graze together. So Abraham suggested that Lot go one way, and he go the other. He gave Lot the choice of which way to go, and his nephew chose the best lands to move into. Abraham was left with the poorest lands for himself and his servants and livestock. At that point the Lord told him to lift up his eyes and look around him in all directions, for He was giving him all the land as far as he could see for his inheritance, promising to bless and increase him abundantly.

This lesson is a good one for us to remember today. When people disappoint us, instead of becoming discouraged and depressed, the Lord wants us to decide to lift up our head and eyes and look around us, trusting Him to lead us into an even better situation because He has one for us. It is so tempting to say, "Oh, what's the use?" and just give up rather than moving in a new direction as Abraham did.

The Lord is constantly exhorting us to lift up our eyes and heads and hearts to take inventory of our blessings and not our problems, to look at Him instead of the evil Satan wants to bring to us because God has plans to bless and increase us abundantly.

No matter how your life has turned out to this point, you have only two options. One is to give up and quit. The other is to keep going. If you decide to keep going, again you only have two choices. One is to live in constant depression and misery. The other is to live in hope and joy.

Choosing to live in hope and joy does not mean you will never have any more disappointments or discouraging situations to face. It just means you have decided not to let them get you down. Instead, you are going to lift up your eyes and hands and head and heart and look not at your problems, but at the Lord, Who has promised to see you through to abundance and victory.

Satan wants to cast you down, but God wants to lift you up. Which will you choose? The "downers" or the "lifters"?

THE HOLY SPIRIT AS A "LIFTER"

*And I will ask the Father, and He will give you
another Comforter (Counselor, Helper, Intercessor,
Advocate, Strengthener, and Standby), that He may
remain with you forever. John 14:16*

Do you know that even the ministry of the Holy Spirit is one
of lifting up?

When Jesus ascended into heaven, He said to His disciples,
"I am going to ask the Father to send the Holy Spirit upon you to
be your Comforter."

The Greek word from which the word "Comforter" is trans-
lated in this verse is *parakletos,*[3] meaning "Ôcalled to one's side,' i.e.
to one's aid...."[4] In other words the Comforter is One Who comes
to stand alongside to encourage, edify, and exhort.

Everything the Holy Spirit does is to keep us lifted up.

Each one of us has to face and deal with disappointments
and discouraging people and situations every day of our lives.
We have been given the Holy Spirit to help us do that. He is our
permanent "pick-me-up" to keep us from becoming depressed.

PRESSING ON OR PRESSED DOWN?

*I do not consider, brethren, that I have captured
and made it my own [yet]; but one thing I do [it is
my one aspiration]: forgetting what lies behind and
straining forward to what lies ahead,*
I press on toward the goal.... Philippians 3:13,14

As I have stated, the word "depression" (or "depress") does
not appear in the *King James Version* of the Bible, so I looked it up

in the dictionary. According to Webster, *depress* means "1. To lower in spirits: SADDEN. 2. To press down: LOWER. 3. To lessen the activity or the force of: WEAKEN."[5]

When Satan comes against you and me to depress us, he is trying to lower our spirits, sadden us, press us down, to lessen our activity and force for God. He is trying to keep us from moving forward, because one of the synonyms of the word "depressed" is "backward."[6]

Satan wants to use depression to "pull our power plug," to drive us backward, while God wants to empower us and propel us forward.

The question is, are we pressing on or are we being pressed down?

THE EFFECTS OF DEPRESSION

One of the dictionary definitions of the word *depression* is "an area sunk below its surroundings: HOLLOW."[7]

Satan wants to drag us down into a sunken position so that we are below everyone else and hollow inside.

The psychiatric definition of *depression* is "a neurotic or psychotic condition marked by an inability to concentrate...."[8]

In extreme depression, a person can become so unable to concentrate he is taken captive by Satan.

In my own life, I have been in such a depressed state I could read the same sentence in a book over and over again and still not grasp what it was saying. Why? Because my mind was not functioning properly.

Dullness, "inability to concentrate, insomnia, and feelings of dejection and guilt,"[9] and even a complete or partial withdrawal from society are all symptoms of extreme depression.

I became so depressed at times I didn't want to see anyone or even get dressed. I just wanted to sit in a dark room all alone and feel sorry for myself. The only thing I would do to pass the time was watch some tearjerker movie on television that would set me on a crying jag all night long.

In fact, when Dave and I first married I became so depressed I thought I wanted to commit suicide. So I made an appointment to talk about it with my pastor.

When we met, I had carefully groomed myself for the occasion, as I always do when I go out. As soon as I walked into his office, I said, "Pastor, I just think I'm going to kill myself."

"No, you're not," he said.

"Oh, yes I am," I answered.

"No, you're not," he repeated. "People who are planning to commit suicide don't go to the trouble to comb their hair, put on makeup, and get all dressed up."

So he totally popped my bubble.

What I was suffering from was not suicidal depression, but simply a milder more miserable form brought on by listening to the enemy instead of listening to the Lord.

CAUSES OF DEPRESSION

What are the causes of depression? There are many. One of them is *guilt*.

Some people are so burdened down with depression brought on by a sense of guilt they have to be hospitalized. In the course of my ministry I have encountered people who are actually in a catatonic state because they blame themselves for something — or everything — that has happened to them in their lives.

One reason we must resist Satan's attempts to pull us down into despair and depression is to avoid ending up in such a state that we have to become hospitalized or we become catatonic. The Word does not promise we will never be attacked by disappointment, discouragement, or any of these other negative emotions, but it does assure us that when they come our way we can successfully defend ourselves against them because we have the Spirit of Truth within us to help us. As we saw before, Psalm 34:19 says, **Many evils confront the [consistently] righteous, but the Lord delivers him out of them all.**

Never assume that just because you are a Christian, you are exempt from attacks by the enemy or beyond the reach of his devices. Just know that when that attack comes, you have the power of God within you to resist and overcome whatever may be sent to destroy you.

Victory comes through recognizing you are being assailed and in knowing what to do to defeat the enemy behind the attack.

The world may be passive, but you and I must be active. The world may operate in the flesh, but we must operate by the Spirit Who lives in us and is there to strengthen, guide, and empower us.

Another cause of depression is *an inferiority complex.*

Every one of us has strengths and weaknesses. We need to face the truth about ourselves, but we must not get down on ourselves because of our human weaknesses. We must simply learn not to keep our attention focused on ourselves all the time. Instead, we must allow the Holy Spirit to direct our minds to whatever truth He wants us to face.

A third cause of depression is *change.*

Many times the reason we have so many problems with our feelings is because some kind of chemical imbalance exists in our body. Now, that does not mean that we should blame every feeling of depression on physical or chemical change, but that is one possible cause to take into consideration.

I have dealt with people who were to the point of being suicidal only to discover nothing was really wrong with them mentally or emotionally, only physically. Once the physical problem was effectively taken care of, they were able to return to a normal life.

In my own life, I have had three major surgeries. Each time I was warned by the medical staff that sometime after being released from the hospital I would probably experience a period in which I felt depressed. That, I was told, is a normal part of our physical makeup.

Although I thought it wouldn't happen to me, and that even if it did I would just rebuke it in the name of Jesus, I did experience it after my first operation. And it was much more of a problem than I had anticipated. The next time I had surgery I was much better prepared to deal with it.

Other medical-type changes include the change of life for women and the mid-life crisis for men. Usually when people have not taken proper care of their bodies in their younger years, in mid-life various problems will begin to develop.

As women experience a loss of the female hormone "estrogen," for example, they may start to undergo changes in their bodies that have a tremendous effect on their mind and emotions.

In somewhat the same way, at a certain age men who have always been in control of their lives may suddenly begin to feel life is passing them by and start acting strangely, which is often just a different form of depression.

Another type of change is that which takes place within our daily routine or existence. Things like changing jobs or moving from one place to another, beginning a new career, or even getting married and starting a family, can bring about emotional stresses that must be dealt with.

Any kind of major change, even a good change like having a baby or retiring from work, can bring on depression, and many times we are not even aware of what is causing the problem.

Another cause of depression is *fear.*

Fearing something gives Satan an open door to intensify the thing causing the fear and make the fear worse. Fear itself is a reaction to change, to the unknown. One thing we must realize is that while fear is a normal reaction to the various changes we all go through in life, it does not have to destroy us. With the help of the Holy Spirit within us, we can learn to face our fear and control it like any other emotion.

As we have seen, among the many other causes of depression are *spiritual issues* such as unforgiveness, self-pity, and chastisement from the Lord. We have also seen that building up huge debt by following our emotions rather than drawing on God's wisdom will cause depression.

Some people have come under depression by resisting or avoiding the call of the Lord on their lives. Instead of going forward with what He has called them to do, they become disobedient and try to live by their own plans and desires. The result is often manifested in a physical, mental, or emotional way as disease or depression.

Whatever the cause of depression — whether it is physical, mental, emotional, spiritual, or some combination of these factors — there is a solution. It is found in the Word of God. Let's look at the example of David, a man after God's own heart, to see how he dealt with this thing called depression.

DAVID DEALS WITH DEPRESSION

> Why are you cast down, O my inner self? And why should you moan over me and be disquieted within me? Hope in God and wait expectantly for Him, for I shall yet praise Him, my Help and my God. Psalm 42:5

In this verse David makes it clear he is having a problem with depression. I would like for us to examine how he handled it, because it shows there is a cure for depression.

As we dissect this verse, we see three distinct things David does in response to his depressed feelings.

He starts out standing to one side looking at his soul which is feeling depressed. First he puts a question to his own soul asking, "Why are you downcast?" Then he gives an instruction to his soul, "Put your hope in God." Finally, he declares what he is going to do, "I will praise the Lord." We might say David has a talk with himself.

We must follow this basic pattern of action as we confront our feelings of depression.

Each of us has been given a free will. We must not allow Satan to take control of that free will, even though that is exactly what he will try to do.

God never tries to take over our free will. The Bible teaches that the Holy Spirit prompts, leads, guides, and directs us. But it never says He tries to force or pressure or make us do something we don't want to do.

Yet Satan is constantly trying to force, pressure, and make us do things we *don't* want to do.

So in our battle against depression and all other negative emotions, one thing we have on our side is our free will.

Now let's look at David's plan for overcoming depression.

PRAISE GOD

We are taught repeatedly that one of the cures for depression is to praise God. When we are depressed, the plan of action to take is to get dressed and go to a praise meeting somewhere so that we can worship and magnify the Lord. We are to listen to praise music and teaching over and over and to sing unto the Lord, making merry in our hearts, regardless of how we may feel.

That is more or less what David is saying to his soul, his feelings. He is saying no matter how he feels inside, he is going to lift his voice in praise and thanksgiving to the Lord, putting his hope in God. By taking action as mentioned earlier like singing, going out around other people, listening to uplifting things, etc., we are "putting on the garment of praise" which Isaiah 61:3 states has been given to us for "the spirit of heaviness."

God provides us with what we need to walk into victory, but we must "put it on" or use it. When we "feel" depressed, we do not "feel" like singing. But if we will do it in obedience to God's Word, we will discover that what God offers us does in fact overcome or defeat what Satan tries to bring against us. In other words, Satan tries to bring us down through sinking, lowered feelings called depression. God lifts us up above depression through singing, hopeful words and inspiring music.

REMEMBER THE LORD

O my God, my life is cast down upon me [and I find the burden more than I can bear]; therefore will I [earnestly] *remember* You from the land of the Jordan [River] and the [summits of Mount] Hermon, from the little mountain Mizar.
Psalm 42:6

When you and I are down, what does the devil want us to remember? Every foul, rotten, stinking thing that has ever happened to us and every shameful, detestable, despicable thing we ourselves have ever done. He wants us to sit there, looking at the floor, taking an inventory of our misery.

At the same time the Lord wants us to raise our eyes and hands and head and heart and sing praises to Him in the very midst of our miserable situation.

Do you remember what King Saul did when he was being assaulted by an evil spirit? He called for David to come play on his harp to soothe his troubled spirit. (1 Sam. 16:14-23.)

Any time you feel your spirit *start* to sink down into depression, you need to take action immediately. Don't wait until you have been in the pit for days before you start to do something to lift your spirit.

When David felt himself sinking, he remembered the Lord and the good things He had done for him in the past. Why did he do that? Because it helped him. It lifted him up out of the miry pit into which he was sliding.

SING, PRAY, HOPE, WAIT, AND PRAISE

> [Roaring] deep calls to [roaring] deep at the thunder of Your waterspouts; all Your breakers and Your rolling waves have gone over me.
>
> Yet the Lord will command His loving-kindness in the daytime, and in the night His song shall be with me, a prayer to the God of my life....
>
> Why are you cast down, O my inner self? And why should you moan over me and be disquieted within me? Hope in God and wait expectantly for Him, for I shall yet praise Him, Who is the help of my countenance, and my God. Psalm 42:7,8,11

When David was down, he said the song of the Lord was with him, a prayer to the God of his life.

Then in verse 11 he went on to say that when his inner self, his soul, moaned over him (as our souls moan over us in self-pity), he put his hope in the Lord, waited expectantly for Him, and praised Him Who was the help of his countenance.

In 1 Samuel 30:6 when David was opposed by his own men who held him responsible for the kidnapping of their families, we read that **David was greatly distressed, for the men spoke of stoning him because the souls of them all were bitterly grieved, each man for his sons and daughters. But David encouraged and strengthened himself in the Lord his God.**

What David did to overcome his heavy depression is what you and I are to do to overcome ours when our souls are bitterly grieved and cast down.

OVERCOME AND RISE UP!

~

...the enemy has pursued and persecuted my soul, he has crushed my life down to the ground; he has made me to dwell in dark places as those who have been long dead.

Therefore is my spirit overwhelmed and faints within me [wrapped in gloom]; my heart within my bosom grows numb. Psalm 143:3,4

What the enemy had done to David is exactly what the devil wants to do to us. He is continually trying to pursue and persecute our soul, crush our life down to the ground, make us to dwell in dark places, overwhelm our spirit causing it to faint within us, and wrap us in gloom so that our heart grows numb.

Satan wants to use our soul, our mind and emotions, to get to our spirit, our heart. He wants to crush the very life out of us so that we become immobile and unable to do anything against his kingdom of darkness.

Although we Christians are subject to the same feelings and emotions, fatigue and stresses that everyone else is, there is supposed to be a difference between us and the world. When people in the world are overwhelmed and give up, we are supposed to overcome and rise up!

How do we do that? By doing what David did in his distress.

REMEMBER, MEDITATE, PONDER, SPREAD FORTH, AND LIFT UP

~

I remember the days of old; I meditate on all Your doings; I ponder the work of Your hands.

I spread forth my hands to You; my soul thirsts after You like a thirsty land [for water]....

> Answer me speedily, O Lord, for my spirit fails;
> hide not Your face from me, lest I become like those
> who go down into the pit....
> Cause me to hear Your loving-kindness in the
> morning, for on You do I lean and in You do I trust.
> Cause me to know the way wherein I should walk,
> for I lift up my inner self to You. Psalm 143:5-8

What is David doing in this passage? He is crying out to the Lord for help.

When you and I feel ourselves sinking down into the pit of depression, we can do what David did here. We can remember the days of old. We can meditate on all the Lord's doings on our behalf. We can ponder the mighty works of His hands. We can spread forth our hands in prayer and supplication to Him. We can call upon Him to answer us speedily because we are leaning on and trusting in Him. We can lift up our soul, our inner being, to Him.

All these things constitute an act of faith, and the Lord has promised to always respond to faith. If we are under a minor attack, it may take only a few hours or days. But if we are under a major attack, it may take a much longer time. But however long it may be, we must stand firm and continue to cry out to God until He hears and answers our plea for help.

Sooner or later the Lord will deliver us, just as He delivered David from all his woes.

Seek the Level Ground
ॐ

> Deliver me, O Lord, from my enemies; I flee to
> You to hide me.

> Teach me to do Your will, for You are my God;
> *let Your good Spirit lead me into a level country* and
> into the land of uprightness.
>
> Save my life, O Lord, for Your name's sake; in
> Your righteousness, bring my life out of trouble and
> free me from distress.
>
> And in Your mercy and loving-kindness, cut off
> my enemies and destroy all those who afflict my
> inner self, for I am Your servant. Psalm 143:9-12

Here in the final verses of this psalm, David calls upon the Lord to deliver him from his enemies because he has run to Him for help and protection. He asks the Lord to teach him His will and to let His Spirit lead him into a level country.

As we have seen, what David was asking for when he spoke of a level country was balanced emotions.

Secure in who he was and in Whose he was, David was able to place himself into the hands of the Lord and allow Him to bring his life out of trouble, free him from distress, punish his enemies, and cause him to win the victory over all those who were afflicting his soul, because He belonged to the Lord.

You and I are to place ourselves in God's hands and allow Him to move on our behalf to win our victory over the devil and withstand his attempts to drag us down into the depths of depression and despair.

FIGHT!

> Blessed be the Lord, my Rock and my keen and
> firm Strength, Who teaches my hands to *war* and
> my fingers to *fight* —

My Steadfast Love and my Fortress, my High Tower and my Deliverer, my Shield and He in Whom I trust and take refuge, Who subdues my people under me. Psalm 144:1,2

Here in the opening verses of the very next psalm, David continues to praise the Lord Who is his Rock, his Strength, Love, Shield, and the One in Whom he takes refuge and Who subdues his enemies.

But notice that David says that the Lord subdued his enemies "under me," meaning that David had a part to play in his own deliverance.

In verse 1, he said it was the Lord Who taught his hands to war and his fingers to fight.

This is the clue to the cure for depression. We must do what David did. We must recognize it, submit it to the Lord, call upon Him for His help, then fight that depression in the strength and power of the Holy Spirit.

How do we fight it? By spending time with God. By speaking His Word. By lifting our eyes, head, hands, and heart and offering the sacrifice of praise and thanksgiving to the Lord, our Rock and Strength, our Love and Fortress, our High Tower and Deliverer, the One in Whom we trust and take refuge, the One Who subdues our enemies under us.

7
HE RESTORETH MY SOUL
ॐ

Thus far in this book we have looked at how not to be led by our emotions, how to find healing of our damaged emotions, how to overcome the unforgiveness that affects our emotions, how to avoid the mood swings that can cause such problems emotionally, and how to defeat the depression that threatens to destroy our whole emotional system.

Now in this chapter we will look at the restoration of our entire souls — our minds, wills, and especially our emotions — as described by David in the Twenty-Third Psalm.

REFRESHING AND RESTORING THE SOUL
ॐ

The Lord is my Shepherd [to feed, guide, and shield me], I shall not lack.

He makes me lie down in [fresh, tender] green pastures; He leads me beside the still and restful waters,

He refreshes and restores my life (my self); He leads me in the paths of righteousness [uprightness and right standing with Him — not for my earning it, but] for His name's sake. Psalm 23:1-3

The Twenty-Third Psalm is so comforting. In it the psalmist David tells us it is the Lord Who leads us, Who feeds, guides, and shields us, Who causes us to lie down and rest, Who refreshes and restores our life, or as the *King James Version* says, our soul.

It is with our soul that our body contacts the world, and it is with our spirit that we contact God. Our soul has a lot to do with our personality, as we have discussed in an earlier chapter.

When David says God leads us in the paths of righteousness, uprightness, and right standing with Him, he is saying God leads each of us in the path right for us individually.

God has a path predestined for each of us. If we will allow Him to do so, He will guide us by His Holy Spirit into the unique path that leads to the fulfillment of His planned destiny for us.

The *King James Version* words verse 3 as, **He restoreth my soul....** As we saw, *The Amplified Bible* words that verse as, **He refreshes and restores my life (my self)....** The word *restore* means, "1. To bring back into existence or use. 2. To bring back to an original state. 3. To put (someone) back in a former position (restore the monarch to the throne). 4. To make restitution of: *give back....*[1] "to return; to cause to return, to restore to a former condition";[2] to refresh.

When David says God will restore our soul, I believe he means God will return us to the state or condition we were in before we erred from following the good plan God had predestined for us before our birth, or before Satan attacked us to draw us out of God's plan for us.

GOD'S PREDESTINED PLAN

For we are God's [own] handiwork (His work-manship), recreated in Christ Jesus, [born anew]

that we may do those good works which God
predestined (planned beforehand) for us [taking
paths which He prepared ahead of time], that we
should walk in them [living the good life which He
prearranged and made ready for us to live].
Ephesians 2:10

God had a good plan laid out for each of us and our life long
before we made our appearance on this planet. The devil comes
to disrupt that plan and to destroy the good thing God has in
mind for each of us.

Since before we were born, God has had a unique plan for
each of us. It is not a plan of failure, misery, poverty, sickness
and disease. God's plan is a good plan, a plan for life and health,
happiness, and fulfillment.

In Jeremiah 29:11 we read: **For I know the thoughts and
plans that I have for you, says the Lord, thoughts and plans for
welfare and peace and not for evil, to give you hope in your
final outcome.**

In John 10:10 Jesus said, **The thief comes only in order to
steal and kill and destroy. I came that they may have and enjoy
life and have it in abundance (to the full, till it overflows).**

It would benefit every one of us if we would say to ourselves
several times a day, "God has a good plan for my life." Why should
we do that? Because each of us needs to be firmly convinced of
that truth to keep us from being affected by our changing circumstances and emotions.

You may be asking, "If God has such a wonderful plan for my
life, why am I not living in it?"

I understand why you would ask that question. It does seem
strange that if God loves us so much and has such good plans for

us, we should have to suffer such misery. What you must remember is that we have an enemy who is out to destroy God's wonderful plan.

Although God had a good plan for my life, I ended up in an abusive environment because the devil came and disrupted that good plan.

But there is something else, something really awesome about God, we need to understand. God doesn't like it when someone hurts us and tries to undermine His plan for us. While He is making us lie down in green pastures to restore our soul, He is getting up to do something about our situation!

It should be a great comfort to us to know that what we cannot do for ourselves, the Lord will do for us — if we will trust ourselves to Him. Only He has the power to restore what has been lost to us, whether that loss was our own fault or the fault of our enemy.

RETURN TO THE POINT OF DEPARTURE

The basic meaning of the word *restore* in this context, as defined in Strong's concordance, is, "to turn back (hence, away)...literally or figuratively (not necessarily with the idea of *return* to the starting point)."[3]

God wants to take us back to the point of departure, the place where we veered from His plan for us, then bring us forward from that place to make things work out the way He intended from the beginning. He will not necessarily take us back to the place physically, and often does not. I don't think He even wants us to try to go there in our memory and relive that experience, although perhaps some people need to do that.

There may be times when people's memories have been blocked by something hideous that happened to them in the past they have not been able to face and deal with mentally and emotionally. In that case, they may need to go back and resolve that situation so that they can move forward with their lives. But as I warned earlier, it is best not to go on a digging expedition.

There are things about my childhood I cannot recall, and it doesn't bother me a bit. There are some things we are better off not remembering and reliving. Many times a God-given ability to forget is a real blessing.

One facet of the ministry of the Holy Spirit is to bring things to our remembrance. (John 14:26.) If there is anything in our past we need to face and resolve, we must trust God to bring it to our attention, so that we don't have to go digging around looking for it.

Some people have been seeking emotional healing for years and years by going back into their sub-conscious and digging up all kinds of harmful and hurtful memories. That is dangerous business. It is much wiser to depend upon the Holy Spirit to bring forth those things that need to be dealt with and put away once and for all.

GOOD FROM BAD
જ

As for you, you thought evil against me, but God meant it for good, to bring about that many people should be kept alive, as they are this day. Genesis 50:20

God wants to restore your soul. Somehow or another, He wants to go back to wherever your life got off track and make everything right from that moment forward.

Although even the Lord cannot change what has happened to you, He can change the consequences of it, as He did for me.

In my own life I cannot truthfully say I am glad I was abused. But because I chose to yield the abuse to God so that He could heal me, He made me a better, stronger, more spiritually powerful and sensitive person.

That is just another example of how God takes what was meant for evil against us and works it out for our good.

Joseph is the one speaking about this in Genesis 50:20 when he told his brothers that what they meant to him as evil when they sold him into slavery in Egypt, God had used for good to save them and their families and many others in time of famine.

OPENING THE ASHES

The Spirit of the Lord God is upon me, because the Lord has anointed and qualified me to preach the Gospel of good tidings to the meek, the poor, and afflicted; He has sent me to bind up and heal the brokenhearted, to proclaim liberty to the [physical and spiritual] captives and the opening of the prison and of the eyes to those who are bound.

To proclaim the acceptable year of the Lord [the year of His favor] and the day of vengeance of our God, to comfort all who mourn.

To grant [consolation and joy] to those who mourn in Zion — *to give them* an ornament (a garland or diadem) of *beauty instead of ashes*, the oil of joy instead of mourning, the garment [expressive] of praise instead of a heavy, burdened, and failing spirit.... Isaiah 61:1-3

Here in Isaiah 61:3 we are told that as part of His restoration process, the Lord gives beauty for ashes. But for that to happen to us, we must be willing to give Him the ashes.

I once saw a movie in which the father of a young woman died. She loved him so much she had his body cremated and kept his ashes in a little box on the mantle. She never intended to keep them there permanently, but was waiting for just the right day to dispose of them.

Finally the perfect day arrived. The wind was blowing strongly as she went to the stable and saddled his favorite horse, the one he used to choose when they went horseback riding together. She directed the horse up to the top of a high hill where she opened the box and threw her father's ashes into the wind which blew them away. That was her way of letting him go — permanently.

That scene came back to me as I was pondering this issue of giving our ashes to the Lord.

You may have been hurt in the past and have kept the ashes of that hurt somewhere close at hand. Every once in a while you may get them out and regrieve over them. If so, I understand because I used to do the same thing.

But you need to do what I did and let go of those ashes, allowing the wind of the Holy Spirit to blow them away to where they cannot be found again. This is a new day. There is no more time left for grieving over the ashes of the past. You have no future in your past.

God has the same good plan for you that He had the moment you arrived on this planet. He has never changed His mind. From the moment the enemy hurt you, God has had your restoration in His heart.

When the Lord placed Adam and Eve in the Garden of Eden, He never intended for them to fall into sin and disrupt His perfect plan for them and their lives. But they did fall into sin and became slaves to Satan.

What was God's response?

Immediately He went to work on His plan for their restoration. He knew He was going to send His own Son to redeem them. That was the whole reason behind Jesus' coming to the earth, as we see in the *King James Version* of 1 John 3:8: ...**For this purpose the Son of God was manifested, that he might destroy the works of the devil.** *The Amplified Bible* version reads: ...**The reason the Son of God was made manifest (visible) was to undo (destroy, loosen, and dissolve) the works the devil [has done].**

MY CUP RUNNETH OVER!

Yes, though I walk through the [deep, sunless] valley of the shadow of death, I will fear or dread no evil, for You are with me; Your rod [to protect] and Your staff [to guide], they comfort me.

You prepare a table before me in the presence of my enemies. You anoint my head with oil; my [brimming] cup runs over.

Surely or only goodness, mercy, and unfailing love shall follow me all the days of my life, and through the length of my days the house of the Lord [and His presence] shall be my dwelling place. Psalm 23:4-6

This last part of David's most beloved hymn of praise to God describes the condition the Lord wants us to be in constantly. He wants us to be protected, guided, comforted. He wants to set a table of blessings before us in the very face of our enemies. He wants to anoint us with the oil of joy instead of mourning. He wants our cup of blessings to overflow continually in thanksgiving and praise to Him for His goodness, mercy, and unfailing love toward us. And He wants us to live forever, moment by moment, in His holy presence.

All these things are part of His good plan for each of us. Regardless of how far we may have fallen, He wants to raise us up and restore us to that right and perfect plan He has for our lives.

BRUISING HEAD AND FOOT

And the Lord God said to the woman, What is this you have done? And the woman said, The serpent beguiled (cheated, outwitted, and deceived) me, and I ate.

And the Lord God said to the serpent, Because you have done this, you are cursed above all [domestic] animals and above every [wild] living thing of the field; upon your belly you shall go, and you shall eat dust [and what it contains] all the days of your life.

And I will put enmity between you and the woman, and between your offspring and her Offspring; He will bruise and tread your head underfoot, and you will lie in wait and bruise His heel. Genesis 3:13-15

After Adam and Eve fell into sin and came before God to answer for their disobedience to Him, the Lord placed a curse upon the serpent who had deceived them and disrupted His plan for them. Among other things, He told him he would bruise the heal of the woman's offspring Who would also bruise his head.

When you were hurt or abused, or when you were simply lead astray by Satan into some kind of sin or failure, those times were the devil bruising your heel. The promise is if he bruises your heel, you can bruise his head.

But you are not going to bruise the head of Satan by sitting around crying over the ashes of your past life. The only way you will ever bruise the head of the devil is by doing the works of God — in spite of everything the enemy may throw at you to stop you.

I believe I am bruising Satan's head every day I live.

Do you want to continually bruise Satan's head, as I am doing in my life and ministry? The way to do that is by helping someone else. Start being a blessing to others, and you will start bruising Satan's head.

Don't just crawl off somewhere to nurse your wounds. Don't just sit and pick your scabs and bleed all your life. Get busy bruising the head of the one who bruised your heel by being a blessing to someone else.

The Bible tells us that the way to defeat evil is by overcoming it with good. (Rom. 12:21 KJV.) But that takes effort and determination. It won't just happen. We have to decide to do it.

For years I did just what I am urging you not to do. I wallowed in the ashes of my past life. When I finally gave those ashes to the Lord, confessing to Him that my life was a mess, and asking Him to set it straight, He called me to work in His Kingdom.

You don't have to have a call like mine to be a blessing. Just get busy being a blessing to each person you come in contact with in your daily life. Start where you are, and God will take you where you should end up.

Maybe Satan has bruised your heel, but if you are willing and determined, you can bruise his head!

Types of Abuse

ॐ

We have said that our soul or our inner being is comprised of our mind, will, and emotions. Often our soul, like our body and our spirit, is abused.

To abuse something is to "misuse" it or "to use wrongly or improperly."[4] In other words, to use it for a purpose other than for what it was intended.

There are several types of abuse: emotional, verbal, physical, and sexual. We will look at each of these separately though they may often occur together.

Emotional Abuse

ॐ

Emotional abuse can occur when a person, who is created by God for love and acceptance, is rejected and made to feel unloved, unappreciated, or unworthy. That kind of treatment will often have an effect on the individual's self-image and self-esteem.

People who are constantly subjected to emotional abuse quickly alter their opinion of themselves and their perspective of others. Their ability to develop and maintain lasting, wholesome relationships with other people is usually affected. They often begin to adjust their behavior toward others because they don't want to run the risk of suffering more emotional hurt and pain.

Verbal Abuse

ॐ

Then there is verbal abuse.

People thrive and grow on edification, exhortation, and encouragement. Words of blessing can motivate people to become all that God intends for them to be.

When you and I were born into this world, God had a ready-made plan tailored just for each of us. He wanted to give us loving, caring parents to nurture us and teach us His Word and provide us everything we needed to live in peace and happiness and security. He wanted us to be brought up in a home in which family members spoke the right things over us and about us and to us, telling us that we could be anything the Lord wanted us to be.

Our heavenly Father never intended for us to be brought up by people who would say to us, "You're never going to amount to anything!" or "Why can't you be like your brother?" or "Why don't you get good grades like your sister?" or "What's the matter with you anyway?"

That kind of talk is damaging to people's souls because it alters their thinking about themselves and others.

If your parents or teachers or other authority figures in your life were constantly telling you such negative things during your formative years, you likely grew up asking yourself, "What *is* wrong with me? Why *can't* I be like my brother? Why *don't* I get good grades like my sister? What *is* my problem?"

I was so verbally abused in my early years that even into my thirties and forties I was still asking, "What's wrong with me?" That continued until the Lord answered my question with, "There's nothing wrong with you, but there is a lot right about you."

He went on to tell me what is right with me is not based on my perfect behavior. I learned I am acceptable to God not because I am so good but because He is so good. I am right with Him because He *chose* to make me right with Him.

The devil doesn't want us to hear the truth. He has offered religion, the following of rules and regulations, to try to get us to make a never-ending attempt to be good enough to deserve God's blessings. The problem is, we can follow all the rules and observe all the laws and still not experience any joy or victory in our lives.

I am not a teacher of religion, I am a teacher of the Word of God. One reason I put so much emphasis on the Bible is that in it we find God's good plan for our lives.

The Bible doesn't teach us about religion, it teaches us about a personal relationship with the Lord Jesus Christ. When He comes to live on the inside of us, we receive His nature in our spirits. (1 John 3:9.) We get an opportunity for a fresh start, a new beginning! **Therefore if any man be in Christ, he is a new creature: old things are passed away; behold, all things are become new** (2 Cor. 5:17 KJV). We are given new life — we literally come alive again.

When that happens, we are empowered to do in our daily lives what we are exhorted to do in Philippians 2:12: **...work out (cultivate, carry out to the goal, and fully complete) your own salvation with reverence and awe and trembling (self-distrust, with serious caution, tenderness of conscience, watchfulness against temptation, timidly shrinking from whatever might offend God and discredit the name of Christ).**

By reading and meditating on the Word of God, we begin to renew our mind, as we are told in Romans 12:2: **Do not be conformed to this world (this age), [fashioned after and adapted to its external, superficial customs], but be transformed (changed) by the [entire] renewal of your mind [by its new ideals and its new attitude], so that you may prove [for yourselves] what is the good and acceptable and perfect will of God, even the thing which is good and acceptable and perfect [in His sight for you].**

Once our mind is renewed by the Word of God, our will begins to come back into line with His will and purpose for us. When that happens, our emotions start to come under control. Our souls are healed so that we can enjoy the righteousness, peace, and joy that are rightfully ours in the Holy Spirit. (Rom. 14:17.)

PHYSICAL ABUSE

Physical abuse includes not only being beaten and mistreated, it also includes such traumatic experiences as being left alone or locked in a closet or even denied outward demonstrations of love and acceptance.

It has been proven that newborn babies who are never touched or held become weak, anemic, and even physically sick. If they are denied loving care and attention long enough, they may actually die.

I have read somewhere that in marriage a woman needs twelve meaningful, loving touches every day from her spouse in order to live out the fullness of her life and be truly healthy and whole. As I was sharing that fact in one of my marriage seminars, a lady on the front row looked at her husband and said, "You're killing me!" She meant he had not been giving her the affection she needed.

The truth is that all of us, no matter what our age, need not only to be safe from physical mistreatment but also to be loved and nurtured physically as well as emotionally.

SEXUAL ABUSE

Finally, there is sexual abuse, which is said to be the worst, most offensive, and most damaging of all.

As designed and instituted by God, sex should be the highest expression of a couple's giving of themselves to each other in love within the bonds of holy matrimony.

When an individual is forced to engage in sex against his or her will, something is taken from that person he or she does not want to share. If that individual is abused in a perverted manner, he or she may suffer lasting damage to the soul as well as to the physical body.

When people, especially children, are abused sexually, their mind, will, and emotions may be tremendously affected. They may become negative, suspicious, critical, judgmental, worried, and unsettled. They may also become what I would call "mentally deep," always reasoning, always trying to figure everything out, always asking, "How can I take care of myself? How can I keep life under control so I don't get hurt anymore?"

"DEEP THINKING"

I was just such a "deep thinker." The problem with it is that a deep thinker never gets to enjoy life.

There are a lot of things in this life you and I are never going to figure out no matter how long and hard we try. We need to retire from self-care and learn to let God do what He wants to do for us and with us in the life He has given us.

Those like me who have been abused in one way or another spend so much of their time trying to avoid being hurt again they neglect other things like building strong, healthy relationships. The fact is, none of us is ever going to have a good relationship with anyone without running the risk of getting hurt.

I love my husband, and as far as I am concerned he is the best husband in the world. But he still hurts my feelings from time to time, just as I hurt his. Sometimes he is not as sensitive as I would like him to be, but then neither am I as patient and understanding as I would like to be.

You and I cannot go through life building walls to protect ourselves from getting hurt by others. When we do that, what we are saying is, "I am not letting you back into my life. I am just going to wall you out." But we must remember that when we wall others out, we also wall ourselves in. We end up living in a prison of our own making. We may be insulated (we think) from being hurt, but we are also insulated from enjoying life and love as we should.

If we insulate ourselves against the rest of the world to protect ourselves from getting hurt, we suffer the pain of loneliness and isolation, as well as the pain of fear.

The walls in our lives must come down, just like the walls of Jericho had to come down so that the Children of Israel could enter in and enjoy their inheritance from the Lord.

Part of tearing down the walls is giving up the endless pursuit of perfection, in ourselves and in others. We must stop trying to make ourselves and everyone else over into our "perception of perfection."

People who have been hurt are always looking for the perfect mate, the perfect children, the perfect house, the perfect neighborhood, the perfect church and pastor, and on and on.

As long as we are in these fleshly bodies we will not find the perfection we are seeking in this life. All of that is part of the emotional ashes we are holding onto and need to give up in order to live in the fullness, abundance, and freedom God intended for us from the beginning.

Rebellion
～

> ...rebellion is as the sin of witchcraft, and stubbornness is as idolatry.... 1 Samuel 15:23

We have seen how abuse affects the mind, but what about the will?

I believe a great deal of rebellion comes from abuse. When a person has been repeatedly hurt by others, there usually comes a time when he makes up his mind, "Nobody is ever going to push me around again. As long as I live, nobody is going to tell me what to do. Why should I submit to somebody I can't trust to do what's best for me? From now on, I'm going to look out for myself and make my own decisions."

So the end result of abuse is often willfulness, stubbornness, and rebellion.

I know from my own bitter experience that being subjected to continual abuse has a lasting effect on a strong-willed person. It was a nightmare for someone of my personality type to be controlled and manipulated for years on end. In my case, the Lord used that experience to make me strong for ministry so that I could help others caught in the same type of situation.

The sad thing is that once people do manage to escape from such an abusive environment, the effects of that abuse do not suddenly end. Many times hurting, wounded people are drawn to other hurting, wounded people. Victims of long-term abuse often marry other such victims. The result is that they end up hurting and wounding each other. Their children pick up the tendency to abuse and pass it on from one generation to the next. The abusive tendency will go on until someone draws the blood-line of Jesus and boldly declares, "That's enough! This curse of abuse is not going any further! It is stopping right here!"

When a decision such as this is made, the will is being used in the way God designed — to choose to follow Him and His way rather than mindlessly following after feelings and emotions.

THE MOUTH AS AN EXPRESSION OF THE SOUL

If anyone thinks himself to be religious (piously observant of the external duties of his faith) and does not bridle his tongue but deludes his own heart, this person's religious service is worthless (futile, barren). James 1:26

For those of us who are born again, the Lord Jesus Christ has done a wonderful thing. He has offered Himself to redeem our soul as well as our body and our spirit.

As we have noted, our soul is comprised of our mind, will, and emotions. Therefore in order to appropriate the full blessing Jesus has purchased for us, we need to understand each of these three vital aspects of our being.

To aid others in this area, my teaching library contains a four-part cassette album ("The Soul" from the "Spirit, Soul, Body" series) on the soul and its three components — plus the mouth, which is the verbal expression of the soul.

Until the mouth is brought under control and submitted to the Lord, it cannot be said that the soul — the mind, the will, and the emotions — is fully redeemed and restored.

Submission as Power Under Control

Be subject to one another out of reverence
for Christ (the Messiah, the Anointed One).
Ephesians 5:21

When I really started studying the Word of God, the Lord
began to deal with me about my willful, stubborn attitude,
especially in the area of submission to authority.

After a time He began really pressing me about the issue. If
you are as thick-headed as I was, you know that sometimes He
has to get very serious with us, as He finally did with me.

One morning as I sat in my pajamas praying for my ministry
to grow, the Lord spoke to me and said: "Joyce, I really can't do
anything else in your ministry until you do what I have told you
to do concerning your husband. You are not showing him proper
respect. You argue with him over minor details, things you should
just let go and drop. You have a willful, stubborn, rebellious
attitude. I have dealt with you about it over and over again, but
you just refuse to listen."

Many of us have this problem. We think we are being obedient to the Word of God, so we wonder why we are not living
in the covenant blessings promised us in it. As we have seen, it is
not enough just to read the Word, or even to learn it and confess
it. We have to be doers of the Word. It is in the doing that the
blessings are released.

I was having problems being submissive because I had such a
strong will, which was the result of having been abused as a child.

Let me give you an example.

One morning I got up and went to take a shower in the new
bathroom Dave had just installed off our master bedroom. Since

he had not yet put up a towel rack, I laid my towel on the toilet seat and started to step into the shower.

Dave saw what I was doing and asked me, "Why did you put your towel there?"

Right away I could feel my emotions getting stirred up.

"What's wrong with putting it there?" I asked in a sarcastic tone.

As an engineer, Dave answered with typical mathematical logic. "Well, since we don't have a floor mat yet, if you put your towel in front of the shower door, when you get out you won't drip water on the carpet while reaching for it."

"Well, what difference would it make if I did get a little water on the carpet?" I asked in a huff.

Sensing the mood I was in, Dave just gave up, shrugged his shoulders, and went on his way.

As it turned out, I did what Dave had suggested, but I did it by angrily slamming the towel onto the floor. I did the right thing, but I did it in the wrong attitude.

God wants us to get to the point of doing the right thing with the right attitude.

As I stepped into the shower after throwing my towel on the floor, I was filled with rage.

"For crying out loud," I ranted to myself, "I can't even take a shower in peace! Why can't I do anything without somebody trying to tell me what to do?"

In my frustration, I just went on and on.

Although I was a Christian and had been in ministry for some time, preaching to others, I myself lacked control over my own mind, will, or emotions. It was three full days before my soul calmed down enough for me to get victory over that bath towel!

What I was lacking in those early days is what many in the Body of Christ lack today: emotional balance and stability.

Emotional Balance and Stability

The development of balance and stability is a part of the restoration of the emotions.

When a person is abused or suffers from feelings of loss, inadequacy, guilt, or failure, not only are his mind and will affected, but also his emotions. But thank God, Jesus came to heal those emotions.

I used to be very unstable emotionally. I would wake up one morning and be all excited because of something I was going to do that day. The next morning I would wake up in the depths of depression because I had nothing to look forward to. Up and down my emotions would go from day to day, hour to hour, or even minute to minute depending on my changing mood.

My husband might come home one day, and I would run to him, throw my arms around him, and kiss and hug him. The next day he might walk in, and I would be ready to throw something *at* him. Most of the time my reaction had nothing to do with anything he had done or failed to do. It was all determined by my own emotional state.

Even if you have never been as abused or as mentally and emotionally unstable as I was, all of us have need of continual restoration in order to maintain proper balance and stability in our lives.

Whatever your past experiences or present circumstances, submit your mind, will, and emotions to the Lord and allow Him to bring wholeness and health to them so that you can fulfill the good plan He has had for you since before you were born.

8
ROOTED IN SHAME
॰ॐ॰

If you know anything at all about gardening, you know that a bitter root produces bitter fruit.

If you have problems in your attitude, behavior, and relationships with others, it is likely a symptom of a deeper problem.

When I was eighteen, I walked away from an abusive situation. I thought since I had physically left behind what was causing me such misery, it would no longer have the power to affect me. But I soon learned that although I did not actually have it in my life anymore, it had me.

Although my outward environment had changed, inside I, myself, had not changed. Even though I was born again and had become a new creation in Christ, in my soul I was still rooted in shame.

A NEW CREATION WITH OLD ROOTS
॰ॐ॰

Therefore if any person is [ingrafted] in Christ (the Messiah) he is a new creation (a new creature altogether); the old [previous moral and spiritual condition] has passed away. Behold, the fresh and new has come! 2 Corinthians 5:17

Some people say, "Since I have been born again, I am a new creation in Christ. Don't bother me with anything about the past because I don't want to hear it. I am dead to all of that. It doesn't affect me any more."

I too have been born again. I too have been made a new creation in Christ. I too believe what the Apostle Paul was telling us here in this verse. But I also think we need to know what it *means* as well as what it *says*.

In order to fully understand what Paul is saying in this verse, I began to study it specifically for this presentation. When I looked up the Greek word translated *new*, I found that it can refer to something consecrated or dedicated for a new or different use.[1]

When you and I are born again, God consecrates or dedicates us to a new and different use, the one for which we were intended in the first place. We might say that we get a fresh new opportunity of service.

When Christ comes to live inside of us, an imperishable Seed is planted within us. Everything we need to be completely healthy and whole is in Him. And if it is in Him, then it is in us. But it is in seed form, and seeds have to be watered and nourished in order to grow and produce fruit.

Two people can be born again at the same time; one will produce great fruit, while the other will produce nothing at all. The reason is that one waters and nourishes the seed planted within him, and the other doesn't.

Why is it that ten years after escaping from the same abusive environment, one person is walking in victory, while the other has made no progress at all? The reason is, one has done what he was supposed to do, and the other has not.

You and I may be born again, but if we do not read and study the Word of God and become doers of it, we will never enjoy all the good things that God intends for us to have. Unless we are obedient to God's Word, the Word will not have any lasting effect upon us.

I was born again. I was a new creation in Christ. I had been given a fresh new opportunity to live for the Lord and produce much good fruit. But instead I was producing rotten fruit. Why? Because although the seed in me was good, the roots were bad.

I was a controller and a manipulator. I was out of control emotionally. I was depressed. I had mood swings. I had a bad attitude, a horrible self-image, and low self-esteem. I didn't like myself or anybody else.

But all of that was not because I wasn't born again or because I had not been given a fresh new opportunity to fulfill God's good plan for my life. The reason was that although I was a new creation spiritually, my soul was still far from being changed.

The sad thing is that I knew how I was. I just didn't know *why* I was that way. I loved God and did not want to displease Him. I loved my husband and did not want to be mean, harsh, or disrespectful to him. I would have loved to be a sweet, gentle, kind, tender, loving wife.

I even agonized over my problem, asking God, "Lord, what's wrong with me?" But no matter how hard I tried to change on the outside and become a sweet-smelling savor to the Lord, on the inside I was filled with rotten fruit that gave off an offensive odor to everyone with whom I came in contact. Although I wanted to be a tree that produced good fruit, I could not do so because I had within me a root of bitterness. And a bitter root always produces bitter fruit.

THE BAD TREE

For each tree is known and identified by its own fruit; for figs are not gathered from thornbushes, nor is a cluster of grapes picked from a bramblebush.

The upright (honorable, intrinsically good) man out of the good treasure [stored] in his heart produces what is upright (honorable and intrinsically good), and the evil man out of the evil storehouse brings forth that which is depraved (wicked and intrinsically evil); for out of the abundance (overflow) of the heart his mouth speaks. Luke 6:44,45

Imagine a tree with its roots, trunk, and branches. Imagine it is a fruit tree in the process of bearing fruit.

Jesus said every tree is known and identified by its fruit. Imagine you are looking at a fruit tree depicting all the bad things produced in the life of an emotionally disturbed individual. If you look at the roots of that tree you will see things like rejection, abuse, guilt, negativism, and shame.

If you have a problem with any of these things in your life, the reason is they are the bitter fruit of what has been rooted into your thinking. You may be the product of improper mirroring and imaging by your parents and others. That is, you may be suffering because of the bad example to which you were exposed continually in your earlier years.

If you were told over and over in your youth by parents, teachers, or other authority figures you were no good, there was something wrong with you, you couldn't do anything right, you were worthless and would never amount to anything, you may have begun to believe it. Satan may have reinforced that message by repeating it in your mind again and again until it became part of your self-image so that you actually became on the outside the way you envisioned yourself on the inside.

It has been proven that if people believe something about themselves strongly enough, they will actually begin to behave the way they perceive themselves to be. What is happening is that the roots of that bad tree imagined in the mind are producing the bad fruit that grew from it.

One of the bad fruits of the bad tree is shame.

Normal Shame and Rooted Shame
∽

My dishonor is before me all day long, and
shame has covered my face. Psalm 44:15

If you are rooted in shame, then you need to be aware that shame is different from guilt, another of the roots of the bad fruit tree you imagined. There is also a difference between normal shame and rooted shame.

For example, if I knock over my water glass in a fancy restaurant, I feel ashamed or embarrassed because I have made a mess in front of everybody. That's normal. But I soon adjust to the mishap and go on. That incident does not mar my life.

In the Garden of Eden after the fall, Adam and Eve were ashamed when they realized they were naked, and so they made aprons of fig leaves to cover themselves. But that too was a normal reaction.

When you and I make mistakes or commit sin, we feel bad about it for a while until we repent and are forgiven. Then we are able to put it behind us and go on without any lasting harm.

But when an individual is rooted in shame, it affects his entire life. He is not just ashamed of what he has done, he is ashamed of who he is.

For example, if a child is sexually abused by her father, at first she may be ashamed of what is happening to her. But if it continues over a period of time, a transition will start to take place. She will begin to internalize that traumatic situation and become not only ashamed of what is happening to her but also ashamed of herself.

She may begin to ask, "What's wrong with me that makes my father do that? What is the flaw in me that causes him to treat me that way?"

A child does not have an adult's capacity to look at what is happening and lay the blame where it should fall. She may not be able to differentiate between what is happening to her and who she is. She may even think her father's abuse of her is her fault, that she is somehow bringing it on herself. If so, her self-image will be totally affected.

I used to be like that. I had been rejected and abused so long that I thought something was wrong with me.

Thank God, He delivered me from all that. Now when I make a mistake, I may agonize over it for a while, as we all do, but I don't go around blaming myself and asking what's wrong with me. I realize that I made a mistake, but I don't become ashamed of myself for not being perfect.

If other people do things to me, I don't automatically assume that it is my fault because I am so unworthy. I don't become ashamed because I think I'm no good, or think I deserve to be mistreated.

The Trunk

If a person is rooted in shame, sooner or later as he moves up the trunk of that bad tree he will, perhaps unconsciously, begin to think, "Because I'm so flawed, the real me is not acceptable, so I'd better put on a pretend me."

How many of us go through life striving to be something we are not, trying to impress everybody, and getting so mixed up and confused we don't know what we are really like anymore?

Often in our fear of being seen for what we really are, we try to be one way for one person or group and a totally different way for another. Because of our fear of rejection or ridicule we spend our entire lives trying to be what we think everybody else wants us to be. In the process we lose track of who we really are and end up completely miserable.

If we feel who we really are is not acceptable, we may begin to hide our true feelings. Some people become so adept at repressing their true feelings they become emotionally frozen, unable to express any kind of feeling or emotion at all because it is too painful to do so.

Many men will not show any vulnerability, tenderness, or sensitivity because they are afraid if they do, they might appear to be weak or wimpish. So instead of baring their true feelings, they put on a "macho" front, which only masks the problem, causing pain for themselves and others, especially their wives.

I think it is time we all came out from behind our masks and became real. It is time to stop role playing. We need to allow the Holy Spirit to teach us who we really are. Then we need to be honest and to open ourselves to others, instead of always being afraid of what people will think of us if we reveal our true nature and character.

OUR "LOVE TANK"
෨

[I pray] that Christ may dwell in your hearts by
faith; that ye, [may be] rooted and grounded in love.
Ephesians 3:17 KJV

Each one of us is born with a "love tank,"[2] and if our tank is
empty, we are in trouble.

We need to start receiving love from the moment we are born
and continue receiving it — and giving it out — until the day
we die.

Sometimes Satan manages to arrange things so that instead
of receiving love, we receive abuse. If that abuse continues, we
become love starved and warped, so that we are unable to maintain healthy relationships. Many people develop addictive
behaviors of different types. If they can't get good feelings from
within themselves, they look for them on the outside.

One of the things we must understand is that people have to
have a certain number of good feelings. We are all created to
have good feelings about ourselves. We cannot go around hurting, being wounded, and feeling bad all the time. We are just not
designed and equipped to live that way. To find those good feelings, many people turn to sex, drugs, alcohol, tobacco, food,
money, power, gambling, work, television, sports, and many other
addictive things. They are simply trying to get those good feelings
they are missing from within themselves and their relationships.

Even many Christians are not getting good feelings from
their relationships. They just go through the motions, not truly
enjoying life because of what has happened to them to deprive
them of what they really need and desire — love.

The good news is that whatever may have happened to us in
the past, whatever we may have been deprived of, we can get it

from the Lord. He is our Shepherd, so we shall not want. (Ps. 23:1.) He has promised not to withhold any good thing from us. (Ps. 84:11.)

If we did not get enough love when we were growing up, or if we are not getting enough love now, we don't have to go through the rest of our life with an empty "love tank." Even if there is not one other human being on this earth who loves us, we are still loved by God. We can become rooted and grounded in His love and not rooted and grounded in those things at the root of the bad fruit tree.

BAD FRUIT
ॐ

We have seen that a bitter root produces a bitter fruit and that some of the fruits of the bad tree are rejection, abuse, guilt, negativism, and shame.

Other fruits of that bad tree are depression, low self-esteem, lack of self-confidence, anger, hatred, self-pity, and hostility.

We have examined some of these fruits like abuse, shame, self-pity, and depression, in detail. Now let's look more closely at what the Bible has to say about the bad fruits of anger and hostility as they relate to the root of shame.

FRET NOT YOURSELF
ॐ

Fret not yourself because of evildoers, neither be envious against those who work unrighteousness (that which is not upright or in right standing with God).

For they shall soon be cut down like the grass, and wither as the green herb.

> Trust (lean on, rely on, and be confident) in the Lord and do good; so shall you dwell in the land and feed surely on His faithfulness, and truly you shall be fed.
>
> Delight yourself also in the Lord, and He will give you the desires and secret petitions of your heart.
>
> Commit your way to the Lord [roll and repose each care of your load on Him]; trust (lean on, rely on, and be confident) also in Him and He will bring it to pass.
>
> And He will make your uprightness and right standing with God go forth as the light, and your justice and right as [the shining sun of] the noonday.
> Psalm 37:1-6

When my husband and I were married more than thirty years ago, my mother-in-law wrote verse five of this passage in the front of the Bible she gave me, not knowing anything about me.

That Scripture was what I needed to live by because I had suffered so much in my past. I fretted so much because of what had been done to me and how it had affected my life, I should have been called "Sister Fret!" I needed desperately to quit fretting and start letting. I needed to commit my way to the Lord and allow Him to bring to pass my complete healing and restoration.

If you are hurting and wounded, if you have lost control of your emotions, if you are reaping the bad fruit of the bad roots in your past, then do as I did: quit fretting and start letting.

Read and meditate on these verses daily. Allow them to minister God's grace, love, and mercy to your troubled soul. Commit your way unto the Lord. Roll and repose your cares upon Him.

Put your faith and confidence in Him. Trust and rely on Him to take away your hurt and pain and restore you to full and vibrant emotional health.

Cease From Anger

> Be still and rest in the Lord; wait for Him and patiently lean yourself upon Him; fret not yourself because of him who prospers in his way, because of the man who brings wicked devices to pass.
>
> Cease from anger and forsake wrath; fret not yourself — it tends only to evildoing. Psalm 37:7,8

Sometimes it is hard not to fret when we have been hurt or even abused by someone who seems to have ended up better off than we are.

I am thinking, for example, of women whose husbands abandoned them to run away with some other woman and who seem to be living happily and successfully despite all the wrong they have done and the pain and misery they have caused.

But this passage says that it is not over yet.

In verse eight the psalmist goes on to exhort us for the third time not to fret ourselves. Since it is repeated so many times, this must be an important point, one we are to heed and learn.

Why are we are told to cease from our anger, to forsake our wrath, and to fret not ourselves? Because it only leads to evil.

Instead of giving in to our troubled emotions and seeking revenge upon those who have wronged us or offended us, we are to be still and rest in the Lord, waiting patiently for Him to act. If vengeance is called for, He will bring it forth. We don't have to avenge ourselves against our enemies, because God will do it for us.

We are not to get angry or try to get even. Instead, we are to remain meek, knowing that in the end we will win.

THE MEEK SHALL INHERIT THE EARTH

ʒ

> For evildoers shall be cut off, but those who wait and hope and look for the Lord [in the end] shall inherit the earth.
>
> For yet a little while, and the evildoers will be no more; though you look with care where they used to be, they will not be found.
>
> But *the meek* [in the end] *shall inherit the earth* and shall delight themselves in the abundance of peace. Psalm 37:9-11

According to verse 9, not only will evildoers be cut off, but those who wait and hope and look for the Lord will inherit the earth. Verse 10 repeats the statement that evildoers will reap the consequences of their wrongdoing. Then in verse 11 we are again told that the meek will inherit the earth.

This is the Old Testament passage Jesus was referring to when He said on the Sermon on the Mount: **Blessed (happy, blithesome, joyous, spiritually prosperous — with life-joy and satisfaction in God's favor and salvation, regardless of their outward conditions) are the meek (the mild, patient, long-suffering) for** *they shall inherit the earth!* (Matt. 5:5).

Are you and I laborers or inheritors? Are we to try to make things right for ourselves, or are we to wait on the Lord and let Him work out things for the best?

Are we to be angry or meek?

Meekness as the Middle Ground

The Greek word translated "meek" in Matthew 5:5 is *praus*, meaning mild or humble.[3] The noun form of this Greek word is *prautes*, meaning mildness, humility, or meekness.[4]

In his dictionary of Old and New Testament terms, W.E. Vine says that "...meekness is the opposite to self-assertiveness and self-interest; it is equanimity of spirit that is neither elated nor cast down, simply because it is not occupied with self at all."[5]

I once heard that according to Aristotle, *prautes* (or meekness) is the middle ground or middle course between emotional extremes. In this case, it describes the balance that is to be maintained in regard to anger.

As we have seen, some people are rooted in bitterness because of things that have happened to them in the past. They allow their bitterness, anger, and hostility to manifest itself in abnormal ways.

I was like that. I had all kinds of pent-up emotions within me, but I didn't know how to release them properly. I didn't know how to give them up to the Lord.

I didn't even know who to be mad at. All I knew was that I was angry, and I was hurt. I was tired of being pushed around and mistreated, and I was determined I wasn't going to take anything off of anybody.

I was angry, but not at the right person. I was mad at human beings, including myself, rather than being mad at the real source of my problem, which was the devil and his demons. (Eph. 6:12.)

But because I was so filled with bottled-up anger and hostility, I was always very near what I call the "explode point." All it took was for someone to cross me or offend me, or for something to go wrong in any way, and I was ready to "blow up."

That is one extreme of anger. The other is never to get angry at anything or anybody for any reason.

Some people are so mousy and timid they just assume no matter what happens to them, no matter how badly they are mistreated, it is their fault and offer no resistance at all.

Because of their poor self-image and their low self-esteem, they actually think they *deserve* to be abused and taken advantage of. As a result, they go through life being apologetic when they should be angry in a balanced way. They are just doormats for everybody — and sponges for everything the devil and his demons want to pour out upon them.

That is *not* what the Bible means by meekness.

TRUE MEEKNESS

Now the man Moses was very meek (gentle,
kind, and humble) or above all the men on the face
of the earth. Numbers 12:3

I believe true meekness is getting angry at the right time in the right measure for the right reason.

The Bible says that when God called Moses to lead the Israelites out of bondage in Egypt, Moses was the meekest man on the face of the earth. In other words, he was able to maintain a careful balance between emotional extremes.

For example, Moses was patient and longsuffering with the Israelites, often interceding for them to turn away the wrath of God against them for their sins and rebellion.

As their God-ordained leader and guide, Moses put up with decades of griping and complaining and insolence from these people who never seemed to tire of testing his patience and endurance.

Yet when he came down from meeting with the Lord on the mountaintop and saw the Israelites bowing down and worshiping the golden calf they had made, he became so angry he threw down the tablets with the Ten Commandments written on them!

There is a time to repress anger, and there is a time to express anger. It is wisdom to know the difference. Moses possessed that wisdom, and so should we.

A meek person is not someone who never shows any anger; it is someone who never allows his anger to get out of control.

Meekness does not mean being without emotion; it means being in charge of emotion and channeling it in the right direction for the right purpose.

ADOPTED BY GOD

May blessing (praise, laudation, and eulogy) be to the God and Father of our Lord Jesus Christ (the Messiah) Who has blessed us in Christ with every spiritual (given by the Holy Spirit) blessing in the heavenly realm!

Even as [in His love] He chose us [actually picked us out for Himself as His own] in Christ before the foundation of the world, that we should be holy (consecrated and set apart for Him) and blameless in His sight, even above reproach, before Him in love.

For He foreordained us (destined us, planned in love for us) to be adopted (revealed) as His own

children through Jesus Christ, in accordance with
the purpose of His will [because it pleased Him and
was His kind intent]. Ephesians 1:3-5

Some people have emotional problems because they are
adopted. Since, for some reason, their biological parents chose to
give them up, they feel they were not wanted or loved.

Instead of looking at themselves in that light, they should
consider that their adoptive parents did want them and did love
them, because they chose them on purpose to become part of
their family.

According to this passage, God did exactly that for you and
me. He chose us, actually picked us out, to be His very own
beloved children. Not only that, but He did it before the foundation of the world. Before we even existed, He chose us and
consecrated us, setting us apart to be blameless in His sight, above
reproach before Him in love.

God ordained us, destined us, planned in love for us to be
adopted and revealed as His own children through His Son
Jesus Christ!

With that knowledge, we should have our "love tanks" filled
to overflowing!

The problem is that many people are love starved. Instead
of finding their sense of value and worth in God, their loving
heavenly Father, they try to get the love they crave from sources
that are never going to meet their need.

In Psalm 27:10 David wrote: **Although my father and my
mother have forsaken me, yet the Lord will take me up [adopt
me as His child]**.

Isn't that wonderful news?

It is so comforting to know that even if we were abandoned

for some reason by our earthly parents, God has chosen us and adopted us as His children — not because of our great love for Him, but because of His great love for us.

Now that we belong to Him, He has promised never to leave us nor forsake us, as others may have done, but to always love and care and provide for us as His very own, beloved children.

THE GOOD TREE

> Either make the tree sound (healthy and good),
> and its fruit sound (healthy and good), or make
> the tree rotten (diseased and bad), and its fruit
> rotten (diseased and bad); for the tree is known
> and recognized and judged by its fruit. Matthew
> 12:33

Just as we looked at the bad tree and some of its fruits, now let's look at the good tree and some of its fruits.

We find these fruits listed in Galatians 5:22,23:

> But the fruit of the [Holy] Spirit [the work which
> His presence within accomplishes] is love, joy
> (gladness), peace, patience (an even temper,
> forbearance), kindness, goodness (benevolence),
> faithfulness,
> Gentleness (meekness, humility), self-control
> (self-restraint, continence). Against such there is no
> law [that can bring a charge].

All these good fruits are produced in the life of the individual who is rooted and grounded, not in shame, but in the love of Christ.

Even if you are rooted in shame and all the other fruits of the bad tree, you can draw the bloodline of Jesus Christ through all that and become rooted and grounded in His love. From that point on, you can begin to grow and develop and become normal, whole, healthy and sound, bearing all kinds of good fruit in your life.

LOVING YOURSELF

...You shall love your neighbor as [you do] yourself. Matthew 19:19

I believe one of the greatest problems people have today concerns the way they feel about themselves. The truth is that many people in our society today have a very bad estimation of themselves.

From my experiences in holding meetings and seminars throughout this country and elsewhere, I have come to realize that many people carry around with them some very bad attitudes and negative self-images. In fact, many of them have carried them so long they don't even realize they have them.

Every so often you and I need to conduct a self-inventory.

Have you done one lately? What do you think of yourself? What kind of relationship do you have with yourself?

No matter where you go or what you do in this life, you are always going to have to deal with yourself. There is no getting away from *you*.

If the Lord commanded us to love our neighbor as we love ourselves, He must have meant that it is as important to love ourselves as it is to love others. But it is not enough to love ourselves, we must also *like* ourselves.

Liking Yourself

You are one person you cannot get away from. If you don't like yourself, you have a serious problem on your hands.

I learned this truth several years ago while I was having a terrible time getting along with other people. I discovered the reason I was having so much trouble getting along with others was that I was not getting along with myself.

If you don't like you, you are going to have a hard time liking anyone else. You may pretend you do. But pretence doesn't alter fact. Sooner or later, the truth will come out.

Every one of us is supposed to be a powerhouse for God, living in balance and harmony within and without. In order to do that, we must have not only the right attitude toward others but also the right attitude toward ourselves. We need to be at peace with our past, content with our present, and sure about our future, knowing they are all in God's hands. We need to be stable, rooted and grounded in the love of God as expressed in His Son Jesus Christ.

Because we are rooted and grounded in love, we can be relaxed and at ease, knowing that our acceptance is not based on our performance or our perfect behavior. We can be secure in the knowledge that our value and worth are not dependent upon who we are or what we think or say or do. It is based on who we are in Christ Jesus.

Secure in our knowledge of who we are in Him, we can give up our masks and facades. We don't have to pretend anymore. We don't have to be phony. Instead, we are free to simply be ourselves — just as we are.

What a joy and a release to know that we don't have to go through life trying to impress others by our brilliance and perfection. When we make mistakes — and we will — we can make whatever changes we need to make without getting all upset with ourselves. We can relax in the Lord, confident that He will see that everything works out right in spite of our faults, our weaknesses, and our failures.

The key word in all this is *relax*. Let go and let God do what is necessary to fulfill His good and perfect plan for you.

You don't have to live day after day with something eating at you. Put your shame-based past behind you, and learn to live in the joy and peace that God has intended for you from the beginning.

SHAME DEFINED

Fear not, for you shall not be ashamed; neither
be confounded and depressed, for you shall not be
put to shame. For you shall forget the shame of your
youth, and you shall not [seriously] remember the
reproach of your widowhood any more. Isaiah 54:4

In this chapter we have examined many different facets of shame and the problems it causes. But exactly what is shame in the biblical sense?

In the Old Testament, one of the Hebrew words used to express the idea of being ashamed means to "be confounded."[6]

According to *Webster's II New College Dictionary*, to *confound* is: "1. To cause a (person) to become confused: BEWILDER. 2. To fail to distinguish: MIX UP (confound truth and lies) 3. To cause to be ashamed: ABASH... 4. To damn."[7]

In turn, to *damn* is to "inflict loss upon... 1. To pronounce an adverse judgment on. 2. To bring about the failure of: RUIN... A. To condemn to eternal punishment: DOOM."[8]

What a hideous word! No wonder the devil has so many people going around damning everything and everybody.

The point is that if a person is rooted in shame, if an individual is ashamed of himself, then he doesn't like himself. That doesn't just mean he doesn't like what he does; it means he doesn't like who he is.

Learn To Like Yourself
ॐ

You and I have to learn to deal with our *do* separate from our *who*.

I don't do everything right all the time, but that doesn't mean I am not a child of God or He doesn't love me. I have made mistakes in my life, and I still make mistakes, but I still like myself.

If you like yourself even if nobody else does, you will make it. But when you start to like yourself, other people will begin to like you too.

Look at yourself in the mirror every morning and say, "I like you. You are a child of God. You are full of the Holy Spirit. You are capable. You have gifts and talents. You are a neat person — and I like you!"

If you do that and really believe it, it will work wonders in overcoming a shame-based nature.

To like ourselves does not mean we are full of pride — it simply means we accept ourselves as God's creation. We all need changes in our behavior, but accepting ourselves as the basic person God created is vital to our progress.

A SHAME-BASED NATURE
⟋

Many people live under the curse of a failure spirit. They can never do anything they set out to do. They are always failing, always messing up, always being disappointed, discouraged, and depressed. They don't like who they are. The reason is that they have a shame-based nature.

For a long time I didn't like my personality. And since my personality is who I am, I didn't like me. I didn't want to be as bold and straightforward as I am. I didn't want to be direct and blunt.

For a long time I tried to be like my pastor's wife, who has a real gift of being sweet and kind and gentle. What I didn't realize is that some people are just born that way.

Because I didn't like my personality and who I was, I tried to change myself, instead of letting God change me. I tried to be like my pastor's wife. I tried to be the perfect woman, the ideal wife and mother who grew her own tomatoes and canned them, made jelly, sewed her family's clothes, and on and on.

It didn't work. I was trying to be something I'm not. Finally, I had to learn to just look myself in the mirror and say, "Joyce, I love you just the way you are, and I am going to get along with you. I am not going to be against you anymore."

When a person has a shamed-based nature, as I did, it becomes the source or root of many complex inner problems like depression, loneliness and isolation, and alienation. All kinds of compulsive disorders are rooted in shame: drug, alcohol, and other chemical addictions; eating disorders like bulimia, anorexia, and obesity; money addictions like stinginess and gambling; problems with the mouth like cursing or uncontrolled gossip; sexual perversions of all kinds; the list is endless.

We have spoken, for example, of people who are such workaholics they can never enjoy life. Unless they are working day and night they feel irresponsible. In fact, some people are like I was; if they are enjoying themselves, they feel guilty about it.

Others feel guilty and blame themselves for everything that goes wrong in their lives.

One of my teaching materials is a two-part cassette album called "Breaking the Cycle of Addictions." In it I explore many of these compulsive addictions that plague so many people today.

One of these compulsive addictions is perfectionism, which can also be shame-based. Some people are tormented by perfectionism because of abuse or some other negative situation in their past. They keep trying to be perfect in order to win the attention and affection they feel they were denied.

Such people set themselves up for failure. They set such high standards for themselves that when they fail, they feel bad about themselves. They make impossible schedules, then make themselves and everyone else miserable because they are constantly rushing around trying to meet them.

Our daughter Sandra struggled with perfectionism. She was such a perfectionist she nearly drove herself crazy. She had such a rigid schedule that everything in her daily routine was timed down to the minute. One time she even caught herself counting the ironing, because she had a precise timetable for when each piece was supposed to be finished!

If anything like a phone call interrupted her exacting schedule, she became nervous and upset. If any of her carefully laid plans went awry, she made herself physically sick with fussing and stewing. To God's glory, He has set her free, and she is now a balanced person.

The problem with perfectionism is that since it is an impossible goal, it sets the person up for an inferiority complex. He becomes neurotic. He assumes so much responsibility that when he fails, he automatically assumes it is his fault. He ends up thinking he is flawed because he cannot meet his unreasonable goals or keep his unrealistic schedule.

Sandra thought something was wrong with her because she could not reach the unrealistic goals she set for herself. She finally learned that what was driving her was demonic pressure and not God's requirements at all.

Sometimes such perfectionism and neuroticism actually lead to self-hatred, which opens the way to all kinds of deep physical, mental, emotional, and spiritual dangers.

All of these terrible things are examples of the bad fruit of a bad tree called shame. But there is an answer to all this. It is found in the Word of God.

A TWOFOLD RECOMPENSE

Instead of your [former] shame you shall have *a twofold recompense*; instead of dishonor and reproach [your people] shall rejoice in their portion. Therefore in their land they shall possess double [what they had forfeited]; everlasting joy shall be theirs. Isaiah 61:7

If you are convinced that you have a shame-based nature or that you are rooted and grounded in shame, that curse can be broken off of you through the power of God.

We have seen in Isaiah 54:4 and here in Isaiah 61:7 that the Lord has promised to remove the shame and dishonor from us so that we remember it no more. He has promised that in their place He will pour out upon us a twofold blessing so that we possess double what we have lost, and that everlasting joy shall be ours.

Take your stand on the Word of God. Become rooted and grounded, not in shame and dishonor, but in the love of Christ, being complete in Him.

Ask the Lord to work a healing miracle in your mind, will, and emotions. Let Him come in and fulfill what He came to do: heal your broken heart, bind up your wounds, give you beauty for ashes, joy for mourning, a garment of praise instead of heaviness, a double honor for a double shame.

Determine that from this moment on you are going to reject the roots of bitterness, shame, negativism, and perfectionism, and nourish the roots of joy, peace, love, and power.

Draw the bloodline of Jesus Christ across your life and boldly declare you are healed from the pains and wounds of your past and set free to live a new life of health and wholeness.

Continue to praise the Lord and confess His Word over yourself, claiming His forgiveness and cleansing and healing.

Stop blaming yourself and feeling guilty, unworthy, and unloved. Instead begin to say, "If God is for me, who can be against me? God loves me, and I love myself. Praise the Lord, I am free in Jesus' name, amen!"

9
UNDERSTANDING CO-DEPENDENCE

"Co-dependence," or "co-dependency" as it is often called, is a popular term these days, not only in Christian circles but in non-Christian circles as well.

In this chapter I would like to examine this problem from my personal perspective and share with you some scriptural truth about it that may help you learn to recognize it and deal with it more effectively.

DEPENDENCE AND ADDICTION

In order to understand co-dependence, we must first understand dependence, which can be thought of as an addiction to behaviors, people, or things.

Though we often think of addiction as being related only to tobacco, alcohol, drugs, or some other harmful substance, that is not the case. People can become addicted to all kinds of things, including other people. It is possible to be addicted to worry, excessive planning, and reasoning, control, spending, and a host of other things, both good and bad.

The problem with addiction is that it is evidence of a lack of balance.

As we saw in 1 Peter 5:8, as believers you and I are to **be well balanced.** Why? Because our enemy, the devil, roams around like a hungry lion, seeking someone to devour. That's why we are told in that verse to resist him in the faith.

I believe excess is the devil's playground. If there is any area in our lives in which we are excessive, Satan will use it to take advantage of us.

In general terms, an addiction is something that a person thinks or feels he must have, something he cannot tolerate being without and will do almost anything to get, including unwise, irrational things done in disobedience to God.

All addictions involve a certain amount of obsessive-compulsive behavior. Let's take a closer look at this term to see what it really means.

OBSESSIVE-COMPULSIVE BEHAVIOR

According to Webster, the word *obsession* refers to an often unreasonable preoccupation with something, or a compelling motivation to do something.[1] The person who is obsessive about something thinks about it all the time and talks about it endlessly. His mind and his mouth are constantly focused on that one thing.

If he thinks and talks about it long enough, he becomes compulsive about it, meaning he feels compelled to do whatever it takes to obtain it.

Let me give you an example from my own life.

At one time I loved frozen yogurt. If I let myself think and talk about it long enough, I could become obsessed with it to the point of feeling compelled to get in my car and drive forty-five minutes just to get a three-ounce serving of it.

That is obsessive-compulsive behavior. It controlled me, I did not control it. I still like frozen yogurt, but in a balanced way.

Now we all do irrational things from time to time. But if our lives are marked by constant irrational actions done to satisfy our human urges and drives, then we have a problem. The devil will play on it, trying to convince us that we cannot control our thoughts and desires, and that there is no way for us to be delivered from our irrational, even harmful, obsessive-compulsive behavior.

It all starts in the mind and the mouth and springs from a lack of balance and self-discipline.

ANSWER FOR OBSESSIVE-COMPULSIVE BEHAVIOR

If the problem starts in the mind and the mouth, then the answer must come from the mind and the mouth!

Walking in God's best is much easier than we imagine. The best way to cure anything that ails us — mentally, physically, emotionally, or spiritually — is to get a list of Scriptures that deal with our particular problem or condition and begin speaking them from the mouth until revelation comes to the mind and heart.

Do you remember our remedy for feelings of being unloved? It was to start each day with the affirmation. "God loves me! He loves me!" The same holds true for anything that bothers or troubles us or causes us pain, worry, or misery.

If we would pay more attention to what is going on in our mind and what is coming out of our mouth, we would experience a great deal more happiness, peace, wholeness, and victory in our life.

Addictions are like any other mental, emotional, or physical problem we may have. They can be cured with the right treatment. Even obsessive-compulsive behavior can be healed through the power of the Holy Spirit and the application of the Word of God.

WITHDRAWAL
෴

Of course, any time an effort is made to overcome an ingrained addiction, there is going to be a certain amount of withdrawal that must be undergone.

When I made the decision to give up fretting, worrying, and reasoning, I went through terrible withdrawal symptoms. Every time I broke down and gave in to my desire to worry, fret, or reason, I *felt* better — for a while. Then I would feel worse because I had failed again and had to start all over.

The same principle applies to mental and emotional addictions as to physical or chemical addictions. Just as a chain-smoker or an alcoholic or a drug addict has to endure a certain amount of withdrawal pain or discomfort in order to break his destructive habit, so we must go through a certain amount of pain or discomfort to break our mental or emotional addictions.

It may even be worse when the thing we are addicted to is another person or group of people.

"PEOPLE, PLACES, AND POSITIONS"
෴

...[What concern is it of yours?] You follow Me!
John 21:22

Long before I ever heard the term "co-dependence," I preached a message on dependence and addiction which I called "People, Places, and Positions."

I preached that message because there was something specific going on in my life at the time I was having to deal with, and I thought others might be going through the same kind of experience.

I had become involved in a relationship with a group of people in a church in which I occupied a place of responsibility and held a position of importance. It was a place I wanted to be in, and a position I wanted to fill, among people I wanted to be associated with. The only problem was that God was calling me to let go of all that and move on to what He had for me next. I did not understand why I was having such a hard time being obedient to God.

Now I know the reason was I was dependent on those people, on that place, and on that position. My value and worth were determined by all those things. I was deriving my sense of security, esteem, and fulfillment from who I was with, where I was, and what I was doing. God was asking me to lay all that aside and take off to the backside of nowhere to start all over again.

Of course, there were promises involved, just as there were when God called Abraham: "If you will obey Me and do this thing I am asking of you, then I will broaden your tent and you will stretch out to the north, and to the south, and to the east and west, and I will bless you and make you a blessing to others..."

But like Abraham, in order to enjoy the promised blessings, I had to give up what I thought was the source of my happiness and security and set out, not knowing where I was headed or what was awaiting me when I got there.

I didn't realize that I had an addiction. I was addicted to and dependent upon those people and that place and position. So for a full year I was disobedient to the call of the Lord.

As we have seen, the addict will do whatever it takes to satisfy his craving, even to the point of doing unwise and irrational things in disobedience to God. That's what I was doing, though I was not fully aware of it at the time.

DEPENDENCE ON PEOPLE

> Thus says the Lord: Cursed [with great evil] is the strong man who trusts in and relies on frail man, making weak [human] flesh his arm, and whose mind and heart turn aside from the Lord.
>
> For he shall be like a shrub or a person naked and destitute in the desert; and he shall not see any good come, but shall dwell in the parched places in the wilderness, in an uninhabited salt land.
> Jeremiah 17:5,6

If your soul feels dry, weary, and parched, it may be because you are putting too much dependence on the flesh and not enough on God.

In my own case, when faced with God's call to leave behind the people, place, and position I was so addicted to and dependent upon, and be obedient to Him, I had to transfer my dependence from man to God. I had to realize that confidence in people, no matter how good they may be or how much we may esteem them, is sadly misplaced.

DEPENDENCE ON GOD

[Most] blessed is the man who believes in, trusts in, and relies on the Lord, and whose hope and confidence the Lord is.

For he shall be like a tree planted by the waters that spreads out its roots by the river; and it shall not see and fear when heat comes; but its leaf shall be green. It shall not be anxious and full of care in the year of drought, nor shall it cease yielding fruit.
Jeremiah 17:7,8

In Philippians 3:3 the Apostle Paul tells us that we are to put no confidence in the flesh. Instead, our confidence is to be in God and God alone. He is the immovable, everlasting Rock. He is the One Who is never going to leave us nor forsake us nor let us down.

In my own life, I reached the point of having to transfer my dependence from other people to God.

I love my husband, and we have a good relationship. One time I started thinking, "Oh, what would I do if Dave died? He is so good to me and helps me in so many ways. What would I do if he were no longer with me?"

The more I thought about it, the more upset and fearful I became. So the Lord had to deal with me about it. He said to me, "I'll tell you what you would do if something happened to Dave. You would go on and do exactly as you are doing right now, because it is not Dave who is holding you up, it is Me!"

It is wonderful to have all kinds of human support systems, but we must always stand firm in God and in Him alone.

That's what Jesus did.

JESUS AS AN EXAMPLE
෴

But Jesus [for His part] did not trust Himself to
them, because He knew all [men];

And He did not need anyone to bear witness
concerning man [needed no evidence from
anyone about men], for He Himself knew what was
in human nature. [He could read men's hearts.]
John 2:24,25

Jesus, our example and our role model, did not trust people,
because He knew human nature. Yet He fellowshipped with
people, especially His disciples. He ate and drank with them. He
laughed and wept with them. He confided in them and shared
things out of His heart with them. They were His friends, and He
cared about them. But He did not trust Himself to them.

I think that means that He didn't become dependent upon
them. He didn't throw Himself wide open to them. He didn't
allow Himself to reach the place of feeling He could not get along
without them. He purposely kept Himself in a position where He
was primarily dependent upon God and God alone.

What the Lord is telling us in such passages as this one is, we
must stay in balance. We must love our fellowman and maintain
good fellowship with him. We must get along with others on a
daily basis. But we must never make the mistake of thinking we
can trust others completely.

There is no such thing as a human being who will never fail
us, disappoint us, or hurt us in any way! That person does not
exist on planet earth!

That is not a judgment against our spouse or family or friends.
It is simply an accurate assessment of human nature. We humans

do not have the ability to be totally trustworthy any more than we have the ability to be absolutely perfect.

Don't put pressure on other people by expecting them to never disappoint you, fail you, or hurt you.

As James tells us: **...we all often stumble and fall and offend in many things...** (James 3:2). That's why we need a Healer — the One Who knows us and what we are going through because He has experienced all the same feelings, emotions, pressures, and temptations that we have, yet without falling into sin as we all do so often. (Heb. 4:15.)

KEEPING A PROPER BALANCE

> But far be it from me to glory [in anything or anyone] except in the cross of our Lord Jesus Christ (the Messiah), through Whom the world has been crucified to me, and I to the world! Galatians 6:14

In this verse the Apostle Paul makes it clear he did not glory in anything or anyone, because the world was crucified to him and he to the world.

What I think he meant was that he kept all things — including people, places, and positions — in proper balance in his life. He was not dependent upon anyone or anything for his joy and peace and victory in the Lord.

If we are not careful to maintain a proper balance in our lives, we may develop addictions and even obsessive-compulsive behaviors Satan can play upon to destroy us and our effectiveness for Christ.

In my case, if I get to the place of feeling I just have to have frozen yogurt every night, or go shopping every day, or have people around me all the time telling me how wonderful I am, then I become addicted to those things. I become dependent upon them to give me the sense of satisfaction and fulfillment I crave. I look to the world to provide me what only God can give me.

DEAD TO THE WORLD, ALIVE IN CHRIST

And set your minds and keep them set on what is above (the higher things), not on the things that are on the earth.

For [as far as this world is concerned] you have died, and your [new, real] life is hidden with Christ in God. Colossians 3:2,3

If you and I allow ourselves to become addicted to things and people, and become dependent upon them, the devil will use them to cause us all kinds of grief. That's why we must keep our eyes on Jesus and not on the things of this earth, as Paul tells us in Colossians 3:2,3. Like Paul, you and I are "dead to this world" — and it is dead to us. We must not look to it for our help, but to the Lord.

One time in one of my meetings I was laying hands on people and praying for them when I noticed a woman about my own age curled up on the floor in a fetal position. She was screaming and crying, "Mommy, I need you! Daddy, I need you!"

At first I was a little hesitant to do anything because I am not a psychiatrist — I am not trained to deal with people on a psychological level.

But then she began crying, "Mommy, don't let Daddy do that!" It became pretty obvious to me that she was regressing to a time in her early life when she had been abused, perhaps physically and sexually, by her father. Her mother must have known about it but not done anything to help her. Both of her parents had likely rejected and abandoned her, so she had been wounded and hurting ever since.

She kept screaming and hollering the same thing, "Mommy, I need you! Daddy, I need you!"

Finally, I had had all I could take. I started telling her, "You don't need your mommy and your daddy! You've got what you need! It's Jesus! Don't cry for something you're never going to have! Hold on to what you've got!"

I kept telling her that until suddenly the Holy Spirit gave her a breakthrough. She started saying, "I don't need my mommy and my daddy! I've got what I need! I've got Jesus!"

I ministered to her for a while and then left her with some other counselors while I went on ministering and praying for others. When I came back in about thirty or forty-five minutes to check on her, she was in complete control of herself and her emotions.

You and I are never going to be whole and well mentally or emotionally as long as we think we have to have some person or some thing. It might be nice to have them, just as it would have been nice for this woman to have had her mother and father. But we don't *have* to have anybody or anything but God to get by!

We need to keep ourselves dependent upon the Lord and not allow ourselves to become dependent on anyone or anything else in this life.

DEPENDENCE ON GOD ALONE

We need to be dependent upon God and Him alone, not dependent upon God and anyone or anything else we think we need to keep us happy.

I used to think I could never be happy unless my ministry grew. But it didn't grow until I learned I could be happy even if it never grew.

The Lord told me then, "Anything you *have* to have besides Me to be happy is something the devil can use against you." Somebody etched that statement on a plaque for me, and I placed it in my bedroom so that it was the first thing I saw when I woke up in the morning. I wanted to remember it so that I would never make the mistake of becoming dependent upon anyone or anything other than the Lord.

In my daily prayer sometimes I say, "Father, there is something I want, but I don't want to get out of balance or ahead of You. If it is Your will, I would like to have this thing. But if it is not Your will, then I can be happy without it because I want You to be Number One in my life."

I believe that if we will keep things in their proper perspective and priority, God can give us a lot more than we could ever have by seeking after things rather than seeking after Him and His righteousness. (Matt. 6:33.)

APPROVAL ADDICTION

And yet [in spite of all this] many even of the leading men (the authorities and the nobles) believed and trusted in Him. But because of the Pharisees they did not confess it, for fear that [if they should acknowledge Him] they would be expelled from the synagogue;

For they loved the approval and the praise and the glory that come from men [instead of and] more than the glory that comes from God. [They valued their credit with men more than their credit with God.] John 12:42,43

Many people never receive God's best for them because they are addicted to the approval of others. Even if they know what God's will is for them, they don't walk in it because they are afraid their friends may not understand or agree.

It is true that not everyone approves of God's moves and methods in our lives.

I was almost totally rejected when I began to follow the will of God for me. It was hard to stand alone against the disapproval of others. During that time I learned what matters is not other people's opinions, it is what God thinks that is important.

In Galatians 1:10 Paul wrote: **Now am I trying to win the favor of men, or of God? Do I seek to please men? If I were still seeking popularity with men, I should not be a bond servant of Christ (the Messiah).**

Don't be addicted to approval. Follow your heart. Do what you believe God is telling you to do, and stand firm in Him and Him alone.

DEFINITION OF CO-DEPENDENCE

Now that we have looked at dependence, which we said is a form of addiction to behaviors, people, or things, let's consider co-dependence.

The *Random House Unabridged Dictionary* defines *co-dependence* as "a relationship in which one person is physically or psychologically addicted as to alcohol or gambling and the other person is psychologically dependent on the first in an unhealthy way."[2]

So a co-dependent is a person who is in a relationship with another individual who is addicted to, obsessed by, or controlled by something harmful or destructive.

For example, when my husband and I were first married, I was addicted to certain emotional feelings like anger. Ninety percent of the time I was mad about something. Because I had been abused in my younger days, I was filled with repressed bitterness and rage. If Dave had not been very secure in his relationship with the Lord and with who he was in Christ, he might have allowed himself to be affected by my attitude and behavior.

If he had done that, we would have had a co-dependent relationship, because he would have been dependent upon me, while I was dependent upon my emotions.

But, thank God, that didn't happen.

One of the best things my husband ever did for me was refuse to allow me to make him unhappy.

If you are in a relationship with someone who is dependent upon drugs, alcohol, or some other harmful substance, and you become dependent upon that person to make you happy, then you have become co-dependent. Although you are not addicted to the habit-forming substance that controls his or her life, you are still affected by it and dependent upon it. Each of you has become co-dependent upon the other.

If you and I are not careful, when we enter into a relationship with another person who has an addiction, we will allow that person to put his or her problem off on us.

Are you in a relationship with someone who is making you miserable by his or her addiction or problem? If so, you need to do something about that situation.

In my case, my husband would not allow himself to become co-dependent with me, because he would not allow me to put my problems off on him. For example, I would get mad at him and want to argue with him, but he would just go his way in complete harmony and peace. I used to get so upset with him because he wouldn't fuss and fight with me I would yell at him, "What's the matter with you? You're not even human!"

Don't allow yourself to become co-dependent with anyone. Don't let other people put their problems off on you. Don't let others make you miserable just because they are miserable.

If you have a family, don't let your spouse or your children control your emotions and steal your joy. Just because they may have made a decision that has made their life miserable doesn't mean you are obligated to join them in their misery. Help them with their problem if you can, but don't fall into the trap of trying to solve other people's problems or make them happy.

It can't be done!

Each of us has a free will given to us by God Himself. Each one of us is responsible for our own happiness. If we choose to allow ourselves to become miserable and unhappy, the problem is ours, not someone else's. In the same way, someone else's choice to become miserable and unhappy is not our fault. None of us is responsible for the happiness of anyone else.

I don't think we understand we can help a person most by not giving in to his or her emotional addictions.

My husband was always kind to me. He loved me, and he showed it. Every day he offered to share his love and joy with me, if I wanted it. But he never forced it on me. I was free to join him in his peace and happiness, and he was free not to join me in my misery and unhappiness.

It is so important that we not allow other people to control and manipulate us into becoming co-dependent with them in their emotional bondage.

If your spouse is angry or unhappy or miserable or sad, the problem is his or hers, not yours. If he or she wants to sit and stew or moan and groan or rant and rave or hold a personal "pity party," you are not required to join it or to subject yourself to it.

I can remember getting so angry at Dave because he wanted to play golf every weekend. I tried everything I knew to make him stop. The more I tried to make him quit, the more he played.

It was maddening.

He would say to me, "Why don't you come with me to the golf course?" But that was not what I wanted. I wanted him to stay home with me. Because I didn't want to go, I didn't want him to go either. But he would go and have a good time, while I stayed home and felt sorry for myself all day. Down deep, I was just being stubborn. But it was my choice and responsibility — not Dave's.

Although I was dependent on certain things to keep me happy, Dave would not allow himself to become dependent upon my happiness. He would not allow himself to become co-dependent with me in my emotional addiction.

THE NIGHTMARE OF CONTROL AND MANUPULATION
⅏

> Then I said, I have labored in vain, I have spent
> my strength for nothing and in empty futility; yet
> surely my right is with the Lord, and my recompense
> is with my God. Isaiah 49:4

Do you have any idea what a nightmare it is to spend your life laboring in vain, spending your strength for nothing, continually trying to keep everything and everyone around you under control?

If you do, then God wants you to understand you can make a decision not to be that way any longer. You can decide not to be a controller and a manipulator.

In the same way, if you have allowed yourself to be controlled and manipulated, you can make a firm decision to break that power over your life.

Co-dependence is not something that can be corrected through prayer alone. It takes a decision and willpower on the part of the one who is caught in it.

If you are addicted to any kind of unhealthy substance such as tobacco, alcohol, or drugs, then you know you have to make some effort to overcome that habit.

The same applies if you are a workaholic, or a spender, or an excessive planner, or a worrier. To break that cycle of addiction, you must do more than just pray — you must also make a commitment to break that habit through the power of God.

Likewise, if you are dependent upon someone else who is addicted to any harmful substance or activity, you must take action. You must determine you are not going to allow that person's problems to cause you to get out of balance.

How can you tell when you are getting out of balance? You can tell because you will begin to lose your peace and joy.

If you are like me, you have spent a great deal of your life trying to control everything and everyone around you in a vain attempt to protect yourself so that you will never be hurt again. You must learn to give up your fruitless efforts, because if you don't, you will end up as I did, having labored in vain and having spent your strength for nothing.

You need to learn what I learned, and that is to quit striving and simply place yourself in the hands of God, looking to Him for your recompense and reward.

FEAR
◡

There is no fear in love [dread does not exist], but full-grown (complete, perfect) love turns fear out of doors and expels every trace of terror! For fear brings with it the thought of punishment, and [so] he who is afraid has not reached the full maturity of love [is not yet grown into love's complete perfection]. 1 John 4:18

As long as a co-dependent is in control, he feels safe. When he loses that control, he feels vulnerable and threatened, so he becomes upset, angry, and defensive.

If that describes you, then you must concentrate on knowing how much God loves you, and that perfect love casts out fear. You don't have to be afraid of losing or of being harmed, because the love of God surrounds you and engulfs you and protects you.

THE SAVIOR COMPLEX
◡

Why do you stare from without at the very small particle that is in your brother's eye but do not become aware of and consider the beam of timber that is in your own eye?

Or how can you say to your brother, Let me get the tiny particle out of your eye, when there is the beam of timber in your own eye?

You hypocrite, first get the beam of timber out of your own eye, and then you will see clearly to take the tiny particle out of your brother's eye.
Matthew 7:3-5

Besides fear, a co-dependent often has a false sense of responsibility. He thinks it is his duty to fix everything. He thinks he has to take care of all those he meets and make sure they feel good and enjoy themselves.

The end result is that the co-dependent usually ends up frustrated and worn out because it is impossible to keep everything fixed and in perfect working order and everyone happy and satisfied.

A co-dependent is really just as guilty as the dependent person. If you are living with a controller, and you try your best to keep that person happy by sacrificing yourself to meet his or her expectations or demands, you are an enabler.

Some people actually become addicted to being mistreated. They become so accustomed to abuse that they think they deserve it. They may also think the abuser's behavior is somehow their fault. That's why they continue to do whatever they can to keep the other person happy so that they will be treated right.

If you see yourself in this description of the co-dependent person, learn to lighten up. Quit taking on yourself the burden of everything and the woes of everybody. Don't get the idea that you must be the savior of the world — that job is already taken! Do what you *reasonably* can for people.

If you are always trying to rescue everybody you come in contact with, you are hurting yourself and them. As long as you are trying to do everything for everybody, you will be frustrated and disappointed, and they will never learn to do anything for themselves.

Don't develop a savior complex. Don't try to usurp the role of Jesus Christ. Don't make yourself personally responsible for other people and their problems. Instead, give first priority to solving your own problems, then you can tackle the problems of others.

CO-DEPENDENCE AND LOW SELF-ESTEEM

A person who is co-dependent usually has a low level of self-esteem and is often lacking in maturity.

Mature people are not emotionally and spiritually devastated by every mistake they make. They are able to maintain some kind of balance in their lives.

Freedom from co-dependence is based upon the development of a sense of value apart from what a person does. If an individual is not co-dependent, he is able to stand alone in Christ.

If you are free from co-dependence, you are not dependent on people, places, or positions. You don't have to be in relationship with any certain person or group of people, or be in any certain place, or occupy any certain position in order to feel safe, confident, and secure.

If you are free from co-dependence, you don't feel you have to be in control of everything and everybody. You can allow others to make their own choices and not feel threatened by them or responsible for them. You don't feel you have to try to solve every problem or satisfy every person.

If you are free from co-dependence, you can stand on your own feet and look to God for your sense of value and worth and not to the opinions of others or to outward circumstances. You are able to withstand being controlled or manipulated.

You are free from the bondage of co-dependence because you know who you are in Christ and trust the Lord to see you through.

TRUST GOD

In my seminars on co-dependence I encourage people to hear from God then do what He says.

If the Lord has placed you in a situation, He is mighty enough to cover you with His grace and to show you the wisest way to handle that situation so that you are not harmed by it.

It may not be pleasant to live in that situation, but you must remember that ours is an enabling God. If you will continue to put your trust in Him, He will see you through to victory.

Even if you are living with a controller or a manipulator or even an ungodly person, don't become discouraged. God can change the meanest and roughest person on earth. He can turn the worst cases around and use them for His glory.

If you are caught in a co-dependent situation, He may lead you to speak up to the controller. He may move you to confront the one who is making your life miserable. If you are afraid to do that, He will give you the courage you need to take a stand.

He will also give you the wisdom and courage not to be mistreated and taken advantage of by that person. If you live with a perfectionist, for example, He will help you not make yourself miserable trying to do the impossible to keep that person happy.

The problem is that if you have let that situation go for years, it will be hard to confront the person.

In my own case, Dave lived with my faults for a long time, but eventually he started confronting me and showing me I needed to change.

It was hard. Even though I wanted to change and do what I knew was the will of the Lord, it took courage and commitment to do it.

With the presence and power of the Holy Spirit within you, it can be done. You can be set free in a safe way by being obedient to the Lord and trusting Him to deliver you.

FAITH OR FEAR?

...For whatever does not originate and proceed from faith is sin [whatever is done without a conviction of its approval by God is sinful]. Romans 14:23

Is it possible to allow someone to control and manipulate us, honestly saying we are doing so in faith? Of course not! We know this type of behavior is rooted in fear, not faith. Faith obeys God, but fear is easily intimidated and finds many excuses for disobedience.

A person who is a perfectionist, a workaholic, or involved in sexual perversion is just as dependent as someone who is addicted to a chemical substance like tobacco, alcohol, or drugs. If we try to meet the needs of that person at the expense of our own needs, we are co-dependent upon that individual.

Suppose, for example, we live with a hypochondriac. If we are not careful, we can become co-dependent upon that person's imagined illnesses.

We all want to have compassion on the ill. We certainly want to be kind and caring toward them. But it may be that they are not really doing their part to get well. They are simply using our concern and compassion as a means to draw attention to themselves. Perhaps they were abused in their past and are trying to get from us what they missed in their childhood.

It is good to help people who have been hurt, but when their emotional needs begin to control us, we are in danger of being led by them and their problems instead of being led by the Holy Spirit of God. If we try to meet the needs of someone else at the expense of never being free to do what we feel we should be doing, we are co-dependent upon that individual and his problem.

If we see that is the case and do nothing about it out of fear or misplaced loyalty, we have become co-dependent. Faith causes us to step out and say or do what God places in our hearts, fear causes us to timidly stay under control and domination.

Remember, people who are starved for attention can use their emotional weakness or sickness to control us. How many times have we heard manipulative people say things like, "I'm old, and you don't care anything about me now," or "I raised you all of your life; I sacrificed to house and clothe you and put you through school, and now you want to just leave me here all alone"?

There is a balance to be maintained in such situations. That balance is the Holy Spirit within us to guide us into the truth of each situation and circumstance in which we find ourselves. He will provide us the wisdom to know when we are to be adaptable and adjustable and when we are to take a firm stand and be immovable.

Always keep in mind that *faith obeys God, fear is easily moved by unbridled emotion!*

CO-DEPENDENT, INDEPENDENT, OR DEPENDENT UPON GOD?

Sometimes we may be the one who is dependent upon someone or something. At other times we may be the one who is depended upon.

We may also become independent. That is, we may decide that we don't need anybody — including God. We may decide to do things our way, not allowing ourselves either to become dependent upon others or to be depended upon.

We can also become co-dependent, as we have described.

Finally, we can become dependent upon God, which is the answer for all these problems of emotional imbalance.

For example, in my younger days I was co-dependent upon the person who was using and abusing me. This individual, who was dependent upon alcohol and other vices, controlled my life completely so that I had no freedom whatsoever.

When I got out of that co-dependent relationship, I became a controller and manipulator myself, trying to make others co-dependent upon me and my need for attention and affection. That was the way I was when I got married and why my husband had to confront me about it.

My problem was an emotional imbalance, a lack of objectivity. Because of my background, I just couldn't judge things properly. I didn't know how to act normally because I didn't know what normal was. I reacted out of my emotions rather than by the common sense, wisdom, and the Word of God in me as a believer.

For instance, if Dave was correcting our children, I would interfere and start taking up for them. Dave would try to tell me he wasn't mistreating them, but because I had been mistreated I had a hard time seeing that. I always wanted to do the correcting because I thought I would do it right. In actuality, at times I would be harder on them than Dave was, but I trusted myself, and I didn't trust him.

I was a "control freak." I always wanted to be in charge of everything because I didn't trust anyone but myself.

Part of what God had to teach me was to trust Him and not my emotions. I had to learn to listen to my common sense that told me Dave was not going to hurt our children or me and that I could trust him with their lives and mine. I had to learn not to be independent, or co-dependent, but dependent upon God.

DETACH, DECIDE, AND ACT

The first step in overcoming co-dependence and becoming dependent upon God is to identify the problem.

Let me give you an example.

Some time ago I had a friend who had a strong personality and an explosive temper. She had a lot of problems with her husband and got mad very easily. I allowed her to control and manipulate me because I didn't want to antagonize her or set her off.

In that case, I needed to identify my problem. Then I needed to detach myself from it. I needed to get away someplace where I could analyze what was going on and take the next step, which was to decide what to do about it.

This young woman would call me quite often and ask if she could come over and talk to me. When she came, she would stay most of the day and disrupt whatever plans I may have had. I would try to tell her that I needed to just be alone with the Lord, but she would ask if she could come over, and I would always give in and say yes.

Although I knew what she was asking me was not best for me, I allowed my fear of her anger to override what I knew was God's will for me. So I would end up doing what she expected me to do rather than what I wanted and needed to do. I was doing whatever it took to keep her "fixed."

I have since learned that what I needed to do in that situation was detach, to say, "Could I call you back in a few minutes? I have some things I need to see about, and then I'll get back with you." Then I could have backed away from that upsetting situation and prayed, "Okay, Lord, what do You want me to do here? Do You want me to adapt and adjust my schedule and let this woman come over for her sake? Or do You want me to stand my ground and do what I had intended to do today?"

It is amazing when you get away from such pressing situations and allow your emotions to settle down how much more common sense and wisdom you can operate in. Then if the Lord tells you to do something you know is going to be hard for you, you can gather the strength and courage to do it.

In this case, if the Lord had told me, "Confront this situation and tell this woman you need to spend time alone with Me," I could have asked for the strength to do that and not have allowed myself to be manipulated or controlled or intimidated by her.

That is the beauty of going to the Lord in prayer. He is always there to help us do what we need to do. Regardless of what we may face in life, we can always identify, detach, and decide. Then the final step is simply to act.

But we must be sure that the action we take is the correct one.

Co-Dependency Recovery Groups

Put on God's whole armor [the armor of a heavy-armed soldier which God supplies], that you may be able successfully to stand up against [all] the strategies and the deceits of the devil.

For we are not wrestling with flesh and blood [contending only with physical opponents], but against the despotisms, against the powers, against [the master spirits who are] the world rulers of this present darkness, against the spirit forces of wickedness in the heavenly (supernatural) sphere.

Therefore put on God's complete armor, that you may be able to resist and stand your ground on the evil day [of danger] and, having done all [the crisis demands], to stand [firmly in your place].
Ephesians 6:11-13

There are many co-dependency recovery groups available today. I would like to share with you some of the benefits and dangers associated with them.

First of all, many of these programs are New Age oriented. They involve concepts and practices that are not scripturally sound.

One example is the handling of anger. Some teach that when a person feels angry, he should get alone in a room and take his anger out on some inanimate object, like a piece of furniture. In my opinion, that is not the kind of activity a Christian should be engaging in.

I recall one Christian lady who shared with me that she had been going to one of these groups for some time. She told me her counselor had her beating on a pillow to take out her frustrations and anger. I had to tell her that as far as I was concerned that practice was not scriptural.

I have a teaching in my tape series titled "Beauty for Ashes" in which I deal with repressed anger from a scriptural viewpoint. In it I point out that as we are told in Ephesians 6:11-13, our battle is not just with our emotions, but with the spiritual forces that play on our emotions.

In the *King James Version* of this passage we are told that we war not with flesh and blood (that is, with our own human nature) but with principalities and powers (that is, with strong spiritual entities).

But even then we cannot fight darkness with darkness. I believe the best way to resist and overcome our powerful spiritual enemies is not by giving vent to our anger and frustration in some fleshly manner, but in yielding ourselves to the power and presence of the Holy Spirit within us.

Another lady told me she was in a co-dependency recovery group in her church. As I listened to her describe the program, I realized that although it had much good in it and was probably helpful to many people, this particular program was not thoroughly Scripture-based. There are also other good programs, but this one was mixing Scripture with worldly ways, which is dangerous!

When I asked her about the program, she answered, "I am really enjoying it and think it is good. But I have some concerns about it." She was really saying God's Spirit was giving her a warning about it.

Then she went on to say, "I hear Christians say, ÔIf you have a problem with co-dependence, the Lord will set you free. Just believe the Word and everything will work out all right.'"

She explained she had suffered a great deal of abuse in her younger years and was not getting full relief from her emotional problems through the program at her church. She wanted to know what I thought of it.

I told her, "I firmly believe that emotional healing is not as simple as saying, ÔYou are a new creature in Christ, so just walk like one.'"

Then I explained that although legally we are new creatures in Christ, experientially we have to face and deal with the bad fruit in our lives that is the result of bad roots from the past.

It is true that the Word of God is truth, and that it is truth that sets us free. (John 17:17; 8:32.) But it is also true we must apply the Word of God, the Word of Truth, to our lives before it can have any lasting effect upon us. We have to allow the Holy Spirit to reveal to us the things in our mind and heart that need to be faced and dealt with in the light of His Word.

In order to be set free, we must know what it is we are being liberated from and how to resist it so that it does not come back.

A SERVANT OF GOD OR OF SELF?

For although I am free in every way from anyone's control, I have made myself a bond servant to everyone, so that I might gain the more [for Christ]. 1 Corinthians 9:19

After dealing with this subject of emotional healing for years, I began to see something that disturbed me. I saw that many people make a religion out of being healed. They establish a little co-dependent religion apart from the Church of Jesus Christ. They label themselves and others as co-dependent, then set up a whole system of beliefs and practices based on their condition and their perceived "cure" for it.

The problem is, such people are so preoccupied with their rituals and practices they never seem to get healed. They just work at it all the time.

If you are part of a co-dependency recovery group, I am not saying you should quit it. I am just warning you not to let it become the center of your whole life. Don't become so involved in it you and everyone else in your life are consumed with nothing but your problem.

Never use your problem as an excuse for bad attitudes or behavior.

If you are enrolled in a program, attend the program and complete the course. Then when it is over, you should "graduate" and get on with your life. Don't spend the rest of your time on this earth centering your attention on something that needs to be faced, dealt with, then put behind you once and for all.

BE TRANSFIGURED BY THE WORD

And all of us, as with unveiled face, [because we] continued to behold [in the Word of God] as in a mirror the glory of the Lord, are constantly being transfigured into His very own image in ever increasing splendor and from one degree of glory to another; [for this comes] from the Lord [Who is] the Spirit. 2 Corinthians 3:18

Another danger of the co-dependency recovery groups is their tendency to label as sickness what is really sin. The Bible does not teach that addictions are sicknesses, but they are sins. They are areas which have been allowed to get out of balance — areas which are not being submitted to the fruit of self-control and which must be brought under control through the help of the Holy Spirit.

There may be rare cases in which some addictive behavior is due to a chemical imbalance or some other physical problem, but those are not the majority of situations. If that door is left open, almost everyone would rather think their problem was something they could not control, rather than taking responsibility for their actions.

If you are involved in or affected by something that is sinful, you need to acknowledge that sin, confess it to God, ask for forgiveness, repent of it, then get on with your life. You don't have to spend the rest of your life feeling guilty. You can be forgiven and completely restored by the mercy and power of God.

I realize that breaking addictions such as alcoholism, drug use, sexual perversion, eating disorders, gambling, etc., is not easy, but I sincerely believe the pattern for deliverance is the same as it is for any other problem or sin. Breaking strong addictions may require extra support from loved ones or additional help from the Holy Spirit, but total deliverance will come by following the Holy Spirit's leading and refusing to live in bondage.

If we are not careful, we will do as carnal people and find an excuse for our sins. The only people who are going to reach spiritual maturity are those who are willing to look into the Word of God, see themselves as they are, then allow the Holy Spirit to lead and guide them in changing that image.

BE DOERS OF THE WORD AND NOT HEARERS ONLY
ॐ

> But be doers of the Word [obey the message], and not merely listeners to it, betraying yourselves [into deception by reasoning contrary to the Truth].
>
> For if anyone only listens to the Word without obeying it and being a doer of it, he is like a man who looks carefully at his [own] natural face in a mirror;
>
> For he thoughtfully observes himself, and then goes off and promptly forgets what he was like.
>
> But he who looks carefully into the faultless law, the [law] of liberty, and is faithful to it and perseveres in looking into it, being not a heedless listener who forgets but an active doer [who obeys], he shall be blessed in his doing (his life of obedience). James 1:22-25

If you and I are to be free from our bondage, whatever it may be, we must become doers of the Word and not hearers only. Otherwise we are deceiving ourselves by going contrary to the truth.

It is the truth and the truth alone that will set us free. In order for that truth to work in our lives, we must be responsible. We cannot try to excuse away our sins and weaknesses. Instead, we must become bond servants to God and not to our human nature. We must be dependent upon the Lord and not upon ourselves, other people, or things.

There are benefits to be derived from emotional healing recovery groups if they are scripturally sound and are led by people who are mature. These benefits include the opportunity to talk with others who are going through or have been through the same type of experience. This kind of shared experience and mutual understanding seem to be important to those who are hurting.

People seem to be comfortable talking with me about their abuse because they know I have been where they are. Frequently they tell me that it gives them hope to know that someone made it through all the pain and misery and is now whole.

It is also good to have a set time each week dedicated to facing some of these deeper issues. It prevents people from pushing them into the background and pretending they are not there. It is good to be accountable to others, and a Holy Spirit-filled, Holy Spirit-led group can provide that atmosphere of non-judgmental accountability.

Healing can also come directly from the Holy Spirit and the Word of God. It does not have to come through any other agent. If God chooses to use an individual or group, that is His choice. But it is important to be sure it is His choice and not a desperate attempt to get help at any cost.

Satan is waiting to destroy those who are already wounded. Often emotionally bruised people are easily deceived. They are hurting so badly, they are likely to cling to anyone and anything that offers them help.

I may sound a bit overprotective, but I would rather be aggressively cautious than see people deceived and brought into worse bondage than they are already in.

The bottom line is this: God is your Helper. He is your Healer. He has a personalized plan for your deliverance. Make sure you know what it is, then begin to walk through it one step at a time.

Don't let your wounded emotions control your decision in these matters. Follow peace and walk in wisdom!

10
RESTORING THE INNER CHILD
~

Another one of the things we have heard a great deal about in recent years is the inner child. I believe that every healthy adult ought to have a child within. By that I mean that each individual should be responsible, yet lighthearted.

GROWING UP TOO FAST
~

> And He called a little child to Himself and put him in the midst of them,
> And said, Truly I say to you, unless you repent (change, turn about) and become like little children [trusting, lowly, loving, forgiving], you can never enter the kingdom of heaven [at all]. Matthew 18:2,3

Do you feel in your childhood you were forced to grow up too fast? If so, you should know that happens to a lot of people. When it does, they lose something, and that loss is detrimental to their adulthood.

As adults we should be able to accomplish things in our lives without feeling burdened. We should be responsible and yet lighthearted enough to enjoy our daily lives, even our work, as we read in Ecclesiastes 5:18: **Behold, what I have seen to be good and fitting is for one to eat and drink, and to find enjoyment in all the labor in which he labors under the sun all the days which God gives him — for this is his [allotted] part.**

In fact, I believe we should be able to enjoy every single thing we do.

Some years ago this fact was brought to my attention because I realized I was past forty years of age, married with four children, and yet I could not say I had ever really enjoyed very much of my life.

John 10:10 tells us Jesus said He came to this earth so that you and I might have life and enjoy it to the full.

Some time ago, I did a series titled "The Lost Art of Enjoying Life," then recently wrote a book on the subject, *Enjoying Where You Are on the Way to Where You Are Going.* I really think we have forgotten how to enjoy life. We need to learn how to be childlike, because if there is one thing a child knows how to do it is enjoy — anything and everything. But when a child is forced to grow up too quickly without being permitted to act out his childhood, the result is often tremendous emotional problems.

I believe people today force their children to grow up too fast. The parents are so anxious for their children to learn to read, write, and get a head start on life, they don't allow them just to be kids. Somewhere we have arrived at the mistaken idea that the more we can cram into a child's mind, the smarter and more happy and successful he will be in school and in life.

Now I am not against educating children! Youngsters should be encouraged to learn quickly and easily and to excel in their studies. But they should not be forced to take on responsibilities beyond their years. They need an opportunity to just be themselves and enjoy life before taking on the heavy burdens of adulthood.

In my own case, I hated childhood. I desperately wanted to grow up so that no one could ever push me around or mistreat me. Whatever childhood was supposed to be, it was stolen from me. What I had as a replacement I did not like or want. So I grew up knowing nothing about being childlike. My memories of being a child were very painful to me.

That's what abuse does: it robs a person of his childhood. The same thing happens when a child is saddled with a responsibility too heavy for him to bear at his age. He may have to take care of a sick parent or fill the place of a missing mother or father in the family. He may be forced to go to work outside the home sooner than he should.

I started working at about age thirteen. I lied about my age, saying I was sixteen. I did it because I needed to take care of myself, to earn my own money so that I wouldn't have to ask anyone for anything. I was determined that nobody was going to give me anything for nothing, because I didn't want to feel obligated to anyone.

I had a worker personality, and still do. The natural worker in me, plus the abuse I suffered, turned me into a workaholic. I felt comfortable, happy, and fulfilled only when I was working and accomplishing something. I didn't know how to relax and enjoy anything.

If I had work to do, I was never able to quit until it was finished. I had not yet learned that work is never really finished. There is always something that needs to be done. Now I have learned to work until quitting time then leave whatever I am doing for the next day.

If you and I don't do that, we open ourselves up to burnout. And once we get burned out, it is very hard to recover.

Not being permitted to play will steal a person's childhood and his enjoyment of adulthood.

For some reason I was made to feel guilty on those rare occasions in childhood when I did play. I always had the feeling I shouldn't be doing it, that I ought to be hard at work. That feeling damaged me. It took me years to get to the point of not feeling guilty if I was having a good time.

One night a few years ago, my son asked me to stop working and come sit down and watch a movie with him on television. I wanted to do that. I wanted to pop some popcorn, open up a couple of sodas, and sit down to enjoy a movie with my son. But I had such a nagging sense of guilt I couldn't enjoy it.

Finally I said to myself, "What's my problem? There's nothing wrong with what I'm doing. I need to spend time with my children like this. The movie is clean, the popcorn is low-fat, and the soda is diet. Why do I feel so guilty?"

The Lord said to me, "Joyce, you didn't do everything today you thought you should do. And you didn't do everything today the way you think you should have done it. Therefore you feel like you don't deserve to have any fun."

My problem was thinking I had to deserve every bit of fun, enjoyment, or blessing that came my way. I needed to learn about God's free gift, His grace and favor.

The good things that come to us in this life are given to us by the Lord. (See James 1:17.) He wants to give them to us. He wants us to enjoy life to the fullest, even when we don't entirely deserve it.

We need to be delivered from our guilt complex, from thinking we have to deserve God's gifts to us. We think we have to earn everything, but God wants us to know we only have to receive and enjoy them in thanksgiving and gratitude.

If we are not enjoying life as we should, the reason is that the devil is trying to steal our joy. One way he does that is by destroying the child in each of us.

SATAN IS OUT TO DESTROY THE CHILD

...And the dragon stationed himself in front of the woman who was about to be delivered, so that he might devour her child as soon as she brought it forth.

And she brought forth a male Child, One Who is destined to shepherd (rule) all the nations with an iron staff (scepter), and her Child was caught up to God and to His throne.

And the woman [herself] fled into the desert (wilderness), where she has a retreat prepared [for her] by God, in which she is to be fed and kept safe.... Revelation 12:4-6

When I began to do a Scripture study of this subject, I saw that Satan is always out to destroy the child. And God is always trying to protect the child.

This principle applies not only to actual children and to the promised Christ Child, but also to the inner child in each one of us. Unless we have a healthy child within us, we cannot play and enjoy life the way God intends.

My husband is a wonderful man, a mighty man of valor. Yet he has a big kid in him. He has always been able to have fun and enjoy everything he does. I used to want to be that way. But I wasn't willing to just cut loose, let go, and enjoy myself.

Dave has always been good about going to the grocery store with me. We would go only every two weeks or so, and because we had a certain, limited amount of money to spend, I had to shop very wisely and carefully.

There I would be with my grocery list, coupons, calculator, my three kids, and my husband, really intense about getting the best deal on everything. The truth is, at that time in my life I was pretty intense about everything. But where I was too intense, too "adult" in my attitude and behavior, Dave was just the opposite. He had all the characteristics of a child. He could even have fun in the grocery store!

Characteristics of a Child

...and a little child shall lead them. Isaiah 11:6

When studying this material, I wrote down two or three pages of notes about the characteristics of a child. One of them is that a child has fun no matter what he does.

Regardless of what a child does, he can manage to find a way to have a good time. He can be punished and made to stand in a corner, and he will make a game out of it by doing something like counting the flowers on the wallpaper.

When my son was younger, I asked him to sweep off the patio, so he took a broom and went outside. Since he really didn't want to do that job, he grumbled a little bit. But a few minutes later I looked out and saw him dancing with the broom. He was sweeping all right, but he was having a good time while he was doing it.

That's where you and I fail as adults. We have all kinds of mundane things to do, things we hate and dread and just want to get over with, but we don't allow ourselves to enjoy them.

Included in this list are religious duties, things we think we are supposed to do to be good Christians. If we approach them as obligations, they become chores rather than privileges.

God wants us to learn how to enjoy these things and to enjoy Him. He wants us to enjoy prayer, Bible study, and going to church, just as He wants us to enjoy our spouse, children, family, home, and everything else in life. He wants us to enjoy cleaning house, washing the car, mowing the lawn, and all those other things that we do while thinking to ourselves, "Boy, I'll be glad when this is over so I can do something fun."

For too long we have put off enjoying life. God wants us to enjoy everything — even going to the grocery store.

HAVING FUN

I know that there is nothing better for them
than to be glad and to get and do good as long
as they live;
And also that every man should eat and drink
and enjoy the good of all his labor — it is the gift
of God. Ecclesiastes 3:12,13

So Dave would go to the grocery store with me to have fun. He would chase the kids up and down the aisles with the shopping cart. Since I was so concerned about appearance and reputation, I would try to get him to stop.

"Will you quit making a scene?" I would say. "Everybody's looking at us!"

Then he would answer, "If you don't be quiet, I'll chase you with the cart." Then he would start after me, and I would really get upset. But even then, he wouldn't let me make him mad. Instead he would think up some other way to amuse himself and the kids.

Since he is six feet, five inches tall, he can see over the aisles I can't. He would see me in the next aisle — all intense with my coupons, calculator, and cart — and throw something over the top of the aisle aiming at the cart.

One time I got so upset with him I yelled, "Would you please stop it! You're driving me nuts!"

"Oh, for crying out loud, Joyce," he said. "I'm just trying to have a little fun."

"Well, I didn't come here to have fun," I answered honestly. "I came to get groceries. I want to get them off the shelf, put them in the cart, take them to the checkout stand, haul them out to the trunk of the car, take them home, and put them in the cupboard."

I had my plan all laid out. But in that plan I had not allowed for any fun.

LIVE A LITTLE
ॐ

A happy heart is good medicine and a cheerful
mind works healing, but a broken spirit dries up
the bones. Proverbs 17:22

Wouldn't it be wonderful if we all got around to doing a little living while were going through this life doing all the things we think we are supposed to do?

Because my childhood had been stolen from me, I never learned to be childlike. I never learned to "lighten up" and "live a little." I was always uptight about everything.

But Dave was the type who enjoyed life regardless of what was going on around him. Although I may never have the ability to be like him because of the differences in our personalities, I have learned I can be much happier and more lighthearted than I was.

As a minister of the Gospel, I have a huge responsibility. I have to work hard at what I have been called to do, and I love it. I really do enjoy my work. But if I am not careful, I can become stressed and burned out. That's why I have to make an effort to apply verses like Proverbs 17:22 and develop a happy heart and a cheerful mind.

If you and I are not emotionally balanced, our entire lives will be affected. I truly believe if we don't learn to laugh more, we are going to get into serious trouble. Because, as the Bible teaches, laughter is like medicine. There have been many articles written in recent years stating that medical science now confirms laughter can be instrumental in bringing healing to the body. Laughter is like internal jogging — in many ways as good as physical exercise.

We all need to laugh more. But sometimes we have to do it on purpose.

We have seen how children enjoy life, how they make a game of everything. Another thing they do is giggle all the time. I have seen this in my grandchildren. As they run and play throughout the house, everything they do is punctuated by giggles.

Now I realize that as adults we are not supposed to go through life giggling like children. If we did, we might get fired from our job or, even worse, get sent to a mental facility for examination.

The point I am making is, if we get too serious, we can cause damage to ourselves and to those with whom we come in contact. We need a balance of fun and responsibility.

In my own life, I was so serious I thought I couldn't or shouldn't have anything to do with anything I considered frivolous. It was very hard to get me to laugh at anything. But for a child, it doesn't take very much at all. To him, everything is funny.

We need to find more humor in our everyday lives. And one of the first things we need to learn to laugh at is ourselves. Instead of getting all upset at our human mistakes and shortcomings, we need to learn to laugh at our failures and foibles.

There is nothing funnier than human beings. As Art Linkletter used to say on his old radio and television shows, "People are funny!" And that includes us. We need to recognize that fact and become more attuned to the playful child within each of us.

GOD GAVE US A CHILD

When they saw the star, they were thrilled with ecstatic joy.

And on going into the house, they saw the Child with Mary His mother, and they fell down and worshiped Him. Then opening their treasure bags, they presented to Him gifts — gold and frankincense and myrrh.

And receiving an answer to their asking, they were divinely instructed and warned in a dream not to go back to Herod; so they departed to their own country by a different way.

Now after they had gone, behold, an angel of the Lord appeared to Joseph in a dream and said, Get up! [Tenderly] take unto you the young Child and His mother and flee to Egypt; and remain there till I tell you [otherwise], for Herod intends to search for the Child in order to destroy Him. Matthew 2:10-13

We recognize this passage as part of the Christmas story. The Child spoken of here is Baby Jesus, and those who came and fell down and worshiped Him, presenting Him gifts of gold, frankincense, and myrrh, are, of course, the Wise Men.

I am recalling this story because I want to emphasize the point that when God looked down from heaven and saw our lost condition, His answer was to send us a Child, as we read in Isaiah 9:6: **For to us a Child is born, to us a Son is given; and the government shall be upon His shoulder, and His name shall be called Wonderful Counselor, Mighty God, Everlasting Father [of Eternity], Prince of Peace.**

The Father sent us a Child to deliver us, and right away King Herod set out to destroy that Child.

In the same way, God has given each of us an inner child, and the enemy has set out to destroy that child within us.

The devil is after our childlikeness. He does not want us to be free like little children.

CHILDREN ARE FREE

We have considered some of the characteristics of a child.

One of the most important of these traits is that children are free. They are not concerned with what people think.

Some time ago I watched two young children during a church service. The little boy had brought his toy microphone with him. He was all dressed up in his Sunday suit and during the praise and worship part of the service, he was singing into that toy microphone, holding it up and turning this way and that just like he was performing in front of a huge audience.

The mother of the little girl had obviously let her come to church directly from dance class because she was still wearing her ballet costume. While the little boy was singing enthusiastically into his microphone, she was dancing around like a ballerina.

They were thoroughly enjoying themselves, and they didn't care what anybody thought about it. They were not yet old enough to have come under the bondage of, "What will people think?"

Sometimes it takes a great step of faith to overcome our inhibitions and give free expression to our pent-up emotions, regardless of the opinion of others. That's when we need to exhibit and enjoy the freedom of a child.

AVOIDING PHARISEEISM

> Then were our mouths filled with laughter, and our tongues with singing. Then they said among the nations, The Lord has done great things for them.
> The Lord has done great things for us! We are glad! Psalm 126:2,3

I was watching a Christian television talk show in which the participants were talking about the laughing revival that is sweeping the land.

Someone asked the host of the show if he thought it was of God.

"Does it offend your mind?" the host asked.

"Yes, it does," answered the person who had raised the question.

"Well, then," responded the host, "it's probably of God."

I don't know if you ever noticed it or not, but Jesus went around offending people all the time. It sometimes seems He did it on purpose.

In Matthew 15:12 we read, **Then the disciples came and said to Him, Do You know that the Pharisees were displeased and offended and indignant when they heard this saying?** Jesus' answer to them was: **Let them alone and disregard them; they are blind guides and teachers. And if a blind man leads a blind man, both will fall into a ditch** (v. 14). Jesus knew exactly how to get to the self-righteous Pharisees.

We must be on our guard against Phariseeism. If the truth were known, the Church today is full of Pharisees.

I used to be one of them.

In fact, I was a chief Pharisee. I was rigid, legalistic, boring, out to impress others, humorless, critical, judgmental, and on and on. I was on my way to heaven, but I wasn't enjoying the trip.

You and I need to get out of our straightjackets. Jesus was not sent into this world to bind us up but to set us free. We need to be free to express our thanksgiving and praise to Him for all the great things He has done, is doing, and is going to do for us.

Now I don't mean by that statement we are to go through life trying to see how ridiculous we can act from daylight to dark. I am not talking about weirdness and fanaticism, I am talking about freedom and joy. I am talking about being liberated from the shackles of pharisaical religion so that we can freely follow the leading of the Holy Spirit.

PROTECT AND PRESERVE THE INNER CHILD
ॐ

And having risen, he took the Child and His
mother by night and withdrew to Egypt

> And remained there until Herod's death. This was to fulfill what the Lord had spoken by the prophet, Out of Egypt have I called My Son.
>
> Then Herod, when he realized that he had been misled by the wise men, was furiously enraged, and he sent and put to death all the male children in Bethlehem and in all that territory who were two years old and under, reckoning according to the date which he had investigated diligently and had learned exactly from the wise men.
> Matthew 2:14-16

Again we see illustrated in this story how the devil seeks after the child in each of us to destroy it.

That's why we must be vigilant not to allow him to destroy that inner child the Lord has placed within us to keep us from giving into and being controlled by our pharisaical nature.

BECOMING, RECEIVING, ACCEPTING, AND WELCOMING A LITTLE CHILD

> Whoever will humble himself therefore and become like this little child [trusting, lowly, loving, forgiving] is greatest in the kingdom of heaven.
>
> And whoever receives and accepts and welcomes one little child like this for My sake and in My name receives and accepts and welcomes Me.
> Matthew 18:4,5

You and I must humble ourselves and become as little children. We must also learn to receive, accept, and welcome the child within us. But some of us have a hard time doing that because we are striving so hard to become spiritually mature.

In one place in the Bible, we are told to grow up into Christ (Eph. 4:15), and here we are told by Jesus to become like a little child. The truth is that we are to do both.

The Lord wants us to grow up in our attitude, behavior, and acceptance of responsibility. At the same time He wants us to be childlike in our dependence upon Him and in our free expression of our feelings toward Him.

A good example is found in Matthew 19:14 in which we read what happened when Jesus' disciples tried to keep children from coming to Him: **...He said, Leave the children alone! Allow the little ones to come to Me, and do not forbid or restrain or hinder them, for of such [as these] is the kingdom of heaven composed.**

"Leave the children alone!" Isn't that a wonderful statement? Just as Jesus received, accepted, and welcomed the little children who came to Him, so we must receive, accept, and welcome the little child God has placed within each of us.

Children need to feel safe and secure and cared for. They need to be able to express their feelings and emotions fully and freely. So do we.

UNSTOP THE WELLS!

Jesus answered and said unto her, Whosoever drinketh of this water shall thirst again:
But whosoever drinketh of the water that I shall give him shall never thirst; but the water that I shall give him shall be in him a well of water springing up into everlasting life. John 4:13,14 KJV

In His conversation with the woman at the well, Jesus said those of us who believe in Him will have within us a well of water springing up continually. But if that well gets stopped up, then we have a problem. Because the water within us cannot flow, it becomes stagnant.

If your life is stale and polluted, it may be because your well of living water has been filled up with stones by the enemy, as was done in Old Testament days.

In 2 Kings 3:19 the Lord told the Israelites who were being attacked by the Moabites: **You shall smite every fenced city and every choice city, and shall fell every good tree and stop all wells of water and mar every good piece of land with stones.**

In those days, stopping up wells with stones was one of the weapons used to defeat one's enemies. Our enemy, the devil, still uses that weapon against us today.

I believe that you and I are born with a nice, clean flowing well within us. As children, we still have that well flowing freely. But through time our enemy, Satan, comes along and starts throwing stones into that well: stones of abuse, hurt, rejection, abandonment, misunderstanding, bitterness, rejection, resentment, self-pity, revenge, depression, hopelessness, and on and on. By the time we have become adults, our wells are so filled with stones that they have become stopped up and no longer flow freely within us.

Every now and then we may feel a little gurgle down inside. But we never seem to experience the full release that is needed for our wells of water to flow freely once again.

It is interesting that when Jesus went to raise His friend Lazarus from the dead, He ordered, **Take away the stone** (John 11:39). I believe the Holy Spirit wants to take away the stones that have been clogging our wells of living water.

When alcoholics and drug addicts speak of getting drunk or high on drugs, they call it getting "stoned." With us it is just the opposite. When we are filled with the Holy Spirit, we get "unstoned" so that our lives can overflow with living water.

LIVING WATER

Now on the final and most important day of the Feast, Jesus stood, and He cried in a loud voice, If any man is thirsty, let him come to Me and drink!

He who believes in Me [who cleaves to and trusts in and relies on Me] as the Scripture has said, From his innermost being shall flow [continuously] springs and rivers of living water.

But He was speaking here of the Spirit, Whom those who believed (trusted, had faith) in Him were afterward to receive. For the [Holy] Spirit had not yet been given, because Jesus was not yet glorified (raised to honor). John 7:37-39

Notice in this passage Jesus did not say that from those who believe in Him there will flow rivers of living water *once in a while.* He said these rivers of living water will flow *continuously.*

That living water is the Holy Spirit. What Jesus was talking about here is the outpouring of the Holy Spirit, which we (who have accepted Jesus as Lord and Savior) have received — the Person and the power of the Holy Spirit in us.

The river of living water flows within you and me. It is not supposed to be stopped up, but it is to bubble up within us and flow out of us. And we can release the power of that living water in an even greater measure by receiving the fullness of the Holy Spirit. (Please write to my ministry at the address in the back of the book to obtain more information about this experience.) What we have to learn to do is to go with the flow.

GO WITH THE FLOW

"Go with the flow" has a double meaning for me because of an incident which I describe in great detail in another of my books.[1]

When my children were small, several times a week, it seemed, one of them would spill a glass of milk at the dinner table. Each time I would immediately fly into a rage and into action to clean up the spill because the milk would run all over the table, down into the crack in the table where the leaf was inserted, and down the table legs.

One day while I was under the table during dinner on all fours in a raging tantrum sopping up the mess, the Holy Spirit ministered to me that all the fits in the world would not cause the milk to run up the table legs and back into the glass. Because my children were small, they were going to spill things. The Holy Spirit taught me just to go with the flow.

From that experience I learned to laugh at things that used to upset me. When things go wrong in our lives, Dave and I have learned to say, "I'm not impressed, Satan, you're not impressing me at all."

I have figured out that if we don't let the devil impress us, then he can't oppress us.

Here is another instance in which we have got to learn to use the weapon of laughter against the enemy.

THE LAUGH OF FAITH

The wicked plot against the [uncompromis-ingly] righteous (the upright in right standing with

God); they gnash at them with their teeth.

The Lord laughs at [the wicked], for He sees that their own day [of defeat] is coming. Psalm 37:12,13

The Bible teaches that the Lord sits in heaven and laughs at His enemies because He knows the day of their defeat is coming.

That is what I call "the laugh of faith."

Do you remember Abraham's reaction in Genesis 17:17 when God told him that his wife Sarah would bear a child in her old age and become a mother of nations?

He laughed.

Then in Genesis 18:10-12 when Sarah overheard the Lord repeating this promise to Abraham, she also laughed.

So when the child of promise was born, Abraham and Sarah did as the Lord commanded and named him Isaac, meaning "laughter." (Gen. 17:19.)

Do you know what I believe that says to us? I believe it says that if we will wait on the promises of God and learn to be inheritors instead of laborers, we will end up laughing. We will be giving birth to Isaacs, not Ishmaels.

LAUGHTER UNSTOPS THE WELLS

And Isaac dug again the wells of water which had been dug in the days of Abraham his father, for the Philistines had stopped them after the death of Abraham.... Genesis 26:18

One of the things Isaac did when he was grown was to unstop the wells of his father Abraham which their enemies had stopped up. We can understand this to mean that laughter and joy in the Holy Spirit will unstop our wells.

You and I don't have to labor over this issue or become extremely philosophical about it. We just need to become like little children.

Regardless of our age, if we are to enter the Kingdom of God we need to become like little children, just as Jesus spoke of in Luke 18:17.

The Kingdom of God is available to us at the moment of the New Birth. But in order to enter into it and enjoy it to the full, here and now, we must become like little children.

It is interesting to note how many times the writers of the New Testament referred to the followers of Jesus as "little children."

For example, in 1 John 4:4, we read, **Little children, you are of God [you belong to Him] and have [already] defeated and overcome them [the agents of the antichrist], because He Who lives in you is greater (mightier) than he who is in the world.**

As I ponder on this verse and others like it, it seems to me that the Lord is pretty intent on teaching us to develop and maintain a childlike mentality. In other words, He wants us to feel and act like His little children. He wants us to have a childlike dependence on Him, believing that, like any good father, He will take care of us, watch over us, and provide for us. He wants us to believe that we can relax and be free in Him.

If you have lost your inner child, then this is the time to get that child back.

CHILDREN ARE SIMPLE AND UNCOMPLICATED

The Spirit itself beareth witness with our spirit,
that we are the children of God. Romans 8:16 KJV

Here again, we are told that we are children, the children of God. If that is so, we need to know what children are like so we will know how we are to conduct ourselves and live our everyday lives. That's why we have been looking at what children are like throughout this chapter.

The last of the characteristics of children we need to consider is their simplicity.

By nature, children are simple and uncomplicated. They are also inquisitive in a healthy way, but they don't get involved in reasoning because it causes too much confusion. They ask a lot of questions, but they don't get mentally and philosophically deep.

As we have seen, John 10:10 tells us Jesus said He came that we might have life and have it more abundantly. He also said the devil comes only to kill, steal, and destroy. One of the things He was referring to was the religious system of the day that kept people in bondage because it was not filled with life, joy, and freedom but only with rules and regulations and reasons.

In John 9 when Jesus and His disciples saw a man who had been born blind, they wanted to know who had sinned to cause him to be blind: the man, himself, or his parents. (vv. 1,2.) Asking that type of question is typical of us. That's the way we are — we always try to figure out everything in our own lives and the lives of those around us. We want an answer for everything.

Then when Jesus anointed the man's eyes, sent him to wash in the Pool of Siloam, and the man came away seeing, the Pharisees called him in and questioned him. They wanted to know Who had healed him and how He had done it. (vv. 6-34.)

Spiritual manifestations and demonstrations are things we humans cannot understand. We don't have to know how Jesus heals in order to be healed or to be instruments of His healing for others. We can be like the man who was healed of his blindness by Jesus. We can say, in childlike simplicity and trust, "I don't know how He did it; all I know is that I was blind and now I see." (v. 25.)

We always want to get so theologically deep about everything. But when we start trying to explain God, we get into all kinds of problems. Children don't try to figure out or explain everything. They just accept things as they are and enjoy them. They are not double-minded. They make up their mind what they want and go after it without being bothered by what others think or say.

Children are persistent. They stick to their dreams and goals longer than adults because they know what they want and are not afraid to go for it. As a result, they don't get as discouraged or depressed as adults do.

Children are not afraid of emotions or of showing them. What they feel on the inside is written all over their faces. If they are happy, excited, or enthusiastic, it shows.

We can let children be an example to us in this way. If we are happy in the Lord, we can and should show it to the whole world as a witness to them.

Become like a little child. Stop worrying, fretting, and getting all frustrated and upset trying to figure and reason everything out. Learn to relax and take it easy.

Make a decision to enjoy the rest of your life. No matter what your situation or circumstances, regardless of your past experiences or future prospects, determine to find a way to bring a little laughter and fun into your life.

If you want to be emotionally whole, find and restore the lost child within you.

CONCLUSION

In this book we have looked at how to manage our emotions so that we can enjoy and use them in the way God intended. God gave us emotions to enjoy the abundant life He wants to give us and to be moved in compassion to minister to others for Him.

Until we learn to manage them, our emotions can be our greatest enemy because Satan will try to use them to keep us from walking in the Spirit.

No matter what has happened to you in the past, God can heal you so that you can look at the world through His eyes and enjoy what He has given and is giving you. The rewards of managing your emotions are great — apply what you have read in this book and learn to enjoy everything you do.

ENDNOTES

Chapter 1

[1] *Webster's Ninth New Collegiate Dictionary* (Springfield, MA: Merriam-Webster, 1990), s.v. "emotion."

[2] *Webster's II New College Dictionary* (Boston/New York: Houghton Mifflin Company, 1995), s.v. "emotion."

[3] Webster's II, s.v. "emotionalism."

[4] Webster's II, s.v. "emotionalist."

[5] Webster's II, s.v. "emotionless."

[6] Based on definitions from James Strong, "Hebrew and Chaldee Dictionary" in *Strong's Exhaustive Concordance of the Bible* (Nashville: Abingdon, 1890), p. 10, entry #974, s.v. "trieth," Psa. 7:9 — "to test (espec. metals)"; Webster's II, s.v. "try" — "to melt...to separate out impurities...."; and William Wilson, *Wilson's Old Testament Word Studies* (Peabody: Hendrickson Publishers, n.d.), s.v. "TRY, TRIAL" — "...to prove, especially metals, often of God, as trying the hearts or minds of men...." Another meaning is "to melt, to smelt metals: specially of gold or silver, to purify with fire...."

[7] Watchman Nee, *The Spiritual Man* (New York: Christian Fellowship Publishers, Inc., 1968), pp. 190,191.

Chapter 2

[1] Based on definition from W.E. Vine, Merrill F. Unger, William White Jr., *Vine's Complete Expository Dictionary of Old and New Testament Words* (Nashville: Thomas Nelson, Inc., 1984), "New Testament Section," p. 401, s.v. "MEEK, MEEKNESS," B. Nouns. No. 1 — "...It must be clearly understood, therefore, that the meekness manifested by the Lord and commended to the believer is the fruit of power...."

[2] *Webster's New World College Dictionary*, 3rd ed. (New York: MacMillian, 1996), s.v. "recompense."

Chapter 3

[1] Webster's Ninth, s.v. "mantra."

[2] Bibliographic citation, *Nurse Practitioner* (May 1994), 19(5): pp. 47, 50-56: "It has been estimated that up to 75% of all visits to primary care providers involve presentation of psychosocial problems through physical complaints."

Chapter 4

[1] Based on definition in Webster's II, s.v. "bitter": "has or is a sharp, acrid, and unpleasant taste."

[2] Webster's II, s.v. "forgive."

[3] Webster's II, s.v. "forgive."

[4] Strong, "Greek Dictionary," p. 33, entry #2127, s.v. "bless," Rom. 12:14.

Chapter 5

[1] Strong, "Greek Dictionary," p. 77, entry #5479, s.v. "joy," John 15:11.

Chapter 6

1 Webster's II, s.v. "despair."

2 Webster's II, s.v. "distress."

3 Strong, "Greek Dictionary," p. 55, entry #3875, s.v. "Comforter," John 14:16.

4 W.E. Vine "New Testament Section," pp. 110, 111, s.v. "COMFORT, COMFORTER, COMFORTLESS," A. Nouns, No. 5, *parakletos*.

5 Webster's II, s.v. "depress."

6 Webster's II, s.v. "depress."

7 Webster's II, s.v. "depression."

8 Webster's II, s.v. "depression."

9 Webster's II, s.v. "depression."

Chapter 7

1 Webster's II, s.v. "restore."

2 Wilson, p. 353.

3 Strong, "Hebrew and Chaldee Dictionary," p. 113, entry #7725, s.v. "restoreth," Psa. 23:3.

4 Webster's II, s.v. "abuse."

Chapter 8

1 Vine, "New Testament Section,", pp. 430, 431, s.v. "NEW," 2 Cor. 5:17.

2 Dr. Robert Hemfelt, Dr. Frank Minirth, Dr. Paul Meier, *Love Is a Choice* (Nashville: Thomas Nelson, 1989), pp. 34, 35.

3 Strong, "Greek Dictionary," p. 60, entry #4239, s.v. "meek," Matt. 5:5.

4 Strong, "Greek Dictionary," entry #4240.

5 Vine, "New Testament Section," p. 401, s.v. "MEEK, MEEKNESS," A. Adjective, *praus*. B. Nouns. No. 1, *prautes*.

[6] Strong, "Hebrew and Chaldee Dictionary," p. 56, entry #3637, s.v. "ashamed."

[7] Webster's II, s.v. "confound."

[8] Webster's II, s.v. "damn."

Chapter 9

[1] Based on definition in Webster's Ninth, s.v. "obsession."

[2] *Random House Unabridged Dictionary*, 2nd ed. (New York: Random House, 1993), s.v. "co-dependence."

Chapter 10

[1] *Me and My Big Mouth* (Tulsa: Harrison House, 1997), pp. 174-77.

Bibliography

Hemfelt, Dr. Robert; Minirth, Dr. Frank; Meier, Dr. Paul. *Love Is a Choice* (Nashville: Thomas Nelson, 1989).

Nee, Watchman. *The Spiritual Man*. New York: Christian Fellowship Publishers, Inc., 1968.

Random House Unabridged Dictionary, 2nd ed. New York: Random House, 1993.

Strong, James. *Strong's Exhaustive Concordance of the Bible*. Nashville: Abingdon Press, 1890.

Vine, W. E.; Unger, Merrill F.; White Jr., William. *Vine's Complete Expository Dictionary of Old and New Testament Words*. Nashville: Thomas Nelson, Inc., 1984.

Webster's Ninth New Collegiate Dictionary. Springfield, MA: Mirriam-Webster, 1990.

Webster's II New College Dictionary. Boston: Houghton Mifflin Company, 1995.

Webster's New World College Dictionary. 3rd ed. New York: MacMillian, 1996.

Wilson, William. *Wilson's Old Testament Word Studies.* Peabody: Hendrickson Publishers, n.d.

About the Author

Joyce Meyer has been teaching the scriptures since 1976 and in full-time ministry since 1980. She is the bestselling author of over 54 inspirational books, including *Secrets to Exceptional Living, The Joy of Believing Prayer,* and *Battlefield of the Mind,* as well as over 220 audiocassette albums and over 90 videos. Joyce's *Life in the Word* radio and television programs are broadcast around the world, and she travels extensively to share her message and her popular "Life in the Word" conferences. Joyce and her husband Dave are the parents of four children and make their home in St. Louis, Missouri.

To contact the author write:
Joyce Meyer Ministries
P. O. Box 655
Fenton, Missouri 63026
or call: (636) 349-0303

Internet Address: www.joycemeyer.org

Please include your testimony or help received from this book when you write. Your prayer requests are welcome.

To contact the author
in Canada, please write:
Joyce Meyer Ministries Canada, Inc.
Lambeth Box 1300
London, ON N6P 1T5
or call: (636) 349-0303

In Australia, please write:
Joyce Meyer Ministries-Australia
Locked Bag 77
Mansfield Delivery Centre
Queensland 4122
or call: 07 3349 1200

In England, please write:
Joyce Meyer Ministries
P. O. Box 1549
Windsor
SL4 1GT
or call: (0) 1753-831102

Books By Joyce Meyer

Knowing God Intimately
The Battle Belongs to the Lord
Secrets to Exceptional Living
Eight Ways to Keep the Devil under Your Feet
Teenagers Are People Too!
Filled with the Spirit
Celebration of Simplicity
The Joy of Believing Prayer
Never Lose Heart
Being the Person God Made You to Be
A Leader in the Making
"Good Morning, This Is God!" Gift Book
JESUS—Name Above All Names
"Good Morning, This Is God!" Daily Calendar
Help Me—I'm Married!
Reduce Me to Love
Be Healed in Jesus' Name
How to Succeed at Being Yourself
Eat and Stay Thin
Weary Warriors, Fainting Saints
Life in the Word Journal
Life in the Word Devotional
Be Anxious for Nothing
Be Anxious for Nothing Study Guide
Straight Talk on Loneliness
Straight Talk on Fear
Straight Talk on Insecurity
Straight Talk on Discouragement
Straight Talk on Worry
Straight Talk on Depression
Straight Talk on Stress

Don't Dread
Managing Your Emotions
Healing the Brokenhearted
"Me and My Big Mouth!"
"Me and My Big Mouth!" Study Guide
Prepare to Prosper
Do It Afraid!
Expect a Move of God . . . Suddenly!
Enjoying Where You Are on the Way
to Where You Are Going
The Most Important Decision You Will Ever Make
When, God, When?
Why, God, Why?
The Word, The Name, The Blood
Battlefield of the Mind
Battlefield of the Mind Study Guide
Tell Them I Love Them
Peace
The Root of Rejection
Beauty for Ashes
If Not for the Grace of God
If Not for the Grace of God Study Guide

By Dave Meyer

Nuggets of Life

Available from your local bookstore.